THE LIFE OF DR. ANANDABAI JOSHEE

THE LIFE

OF

DR. ANANDABAI JOSHEE

A KINSWOMAN OF THE PUNDITA RAMABAI

MRS. CAROLINE HEALEY DALL

GYAN

Published by

Gyan Publishing House
5, Ansari Road
Daryaganj, New Delhi-110002
Phone: 011-47034999, 9811692060
E-mail: books@gyanbooks.com

Distribution Network
gyanbooks.com
India, USA, Canada, UK, Australia, France

ISBN : 978-81-212-9198-9 (PB)
First Published, 1888

2nd Impression 2023

Printed at: Gyan Press, Delhi.

THE LIFE OF DR. ANANDABAI JOSHEE
Author: MRS. CAROLINE HEALEY DALL

THE LIFE

OF

DR. ANANDABAI JOSHEE,

A KINSWOMAN OF THE PUNDITA RAMABAI.

BY

MRS. CAROLINE HEALEY DALL,

AUTHOR OF "THE COLLEGE, MARKET, AND COURT;" "LETTERS HOME FROM COLORADO, UTAH, AND CALIFORNIA;" "WHAT WE REALLY KNOW ABOUT SHAKESPEARE;" ETC.

"We will not say her life was brief
For noble death is length of days;
The sun that ripens autumn's sheaf
Poured on her summer's wealth of rays."

BOSTON:
ROBERTS BROTHERS.
1888.

PREFACE.

THE most difficult task of my life lay before me when I undertook to write the Life of Anandabai Joshee. In copying letters or using material furnished by those who loved her, I have been obliged to moderate the terms of affection and admiration which would have seemed extravagant to those who never saw her, or saw her only after her star "drooped toward its setting."

"I have never seen any one who gave me so distinct an impression of being 'high-born,'" said a lady who knew her slightly. It was however not the record which stretched over two thousand years, which gave dignity to Anandabai's mien, but the high-born consciousness, never absent, that in spirit she was the "child of God."

Without the generous aid of Mrs. Carpenter of Roselle, New Jersey, and of Dr. Bodley, Dean of the Woman's Medical College of Pennsylvania, the two friends who made it possible for Anandabai to seek an education in this country, this book could not have been written. Its rapid sale will reward them in the best way for all the self-sacrifice, hard labor, and bitter grief which their devotion has involved, for we hope through that, to aid the projects of her friend and cousin, the Pundita Ramabai Sarasvati.

Our climate is not friendly to the Hindu. Already the cheek of Ramabai has grown pale and her voice weak. If we love her and would aid her, we must speed her on her way.

I have been obliged to allude to the conduct and published writings of Gopal Vinayak Joshee because they were involved in the history of his wife. I have done it as lightly and as briefly as possible, and I wish to say, that I hardly hold him responsible for the letters to the "Index" and "The Open Court," so great appears to have been the excitement under which they were written. The last of these letters is full of mistakes apart from such statements as might be mere matters of opinion. For instance, he states that he and Dr. Joshee sailed from New York Sept. 9th, 1886. But on this day Dr. Joshee was in the Hospital at Philadelphia and she did not sail until October. Still farther he speaks of receiving "eighty or ninety" pounds, for his homeward journey from Mr. Pattison in London; but as *eighteen* was all that was required to make up the passage money, "eighteen or nineteen" would seem the more likely sum.

He alludes also in this letter to "prejudices" against the "Christians" and meditations upon the "low character" of the English, as if these were shared by Dr. Joshee; but this we all know was not possible.

One day, soon after her arrival in America, Anandabai amused herself at Roselle by writing her own "mental photograph" in one of the Albums commonly sold for that purpose. The student of psychology will be interested in comparing this suggestive sketch with the "psychometric impression" elsewhere alluded to.

In a letter written since his wife's death Mr. Joshee thus alludes to the contents of the eleven trunks which Anandabai carried back to India.

"I have given the contents of Dr. Joshee's boxes to an English school, the founder of which Dr. Joshee greatly admired. They are arranged in a nice glass case and I hope they will be better cared for than they could be by me. It was a painful thing to see them all again."

This school is probably at Poonah, and here I suppose Mr. Joshee deposited all the North American pottery, which Anandabai was so anxious to obtain.

It was not until I had nearly finished my work that I learned that the acquaintance between Ramabai and her cousin began through the cordial entreaty of the Joshees that she would come and live with them at Serampore at a time when she was bitterly persecuted.

The following letter will explain itself.

553 SOUTH 16TH ST., PHILADELPHIA,
Jan. 16th, 1888.

MY DEAR MRS. DALL, — Dear Doctor Joshee was staying in Serampore when she invited me to come to her after my husband's sudden death.

I did not know her personally at that time, but had some correspondence with her.

My husband being of low caste, my marrying him was altogether against the country's custom, and we were despised and shunned by our most intimate friends and relatives.

So much was this the case, that my husband's own brother would not write to him for fear of losing caste.

Under such circumstances, we had no intercourse with many, and were too proud to ask any favors. I therefore resolved to do what I could to take care of my baby and myself independently of all relatives or friends. I made this promise to my dear husband before he left me. Therefore I did not accept Mrs. Joshee's kind invitation to go to her in my distress. I was very grateful to her all the same, for she was the only person in the whole country who cared for me, such an outcast had I become in the eyes of my people. Nor shall I ever cease to be grateful to her for this kindness.

With all good wishes for the New Year,

I am, sincerely yours,

RAMABAI.

It gives me great pleasure to print this letter, for Gopal must have united with Anandabai in giving this invitation, and the action proves him to have been at this time what his wife always believed him to be, — a liberal and tender-hearted man.

It must be obvious to all my readers, that in a Memoir prepared as this has been, there must be more than the usual liability to error in detail. I have done all that I could to prevent such errors, and as the greater part of the book consists of Anandabai's own letters, I hope that no serious error is likely to appear.

Since the Memoir went to press, I have heard

from Mrs. Carpenter and the Pundita Ramabai, that there is every reason to suppose that Anandabai was betrothed to Gopal, by a ceremony considered as irrevocable as marriage, when she went away with him from Kalyan in the company of her grandmother.

Mrs. Carpenter thinks that Anandabai told her this, and the Pundita, who knew nothing of her cousin at that time, is sure that her departure would not have been permitted if she had not been betrothed.

All this may have been so, but if it were it was never even hinted in my conversations with Dr. Joshee. At that time she expected to send me on her return to India some significant extracts from her family history, and a brief outline of her own life. I was not very anxious about details, but tried to understand fully the *character of her mind*, and her individual emancipation from tradition and custom.

She said nothing about betrothal. If betrothed, it is usual for a Hindu woman to pass into the care of her husband's family. Nothing was said about this, only the bitter cry, many times repeated, "I thought I should never learn anything more, and I would rather have died." She never said, nor did I ever ask, whether she and her grandmother lived in the same house with Gopal previous to her marriage, and as it is now too late to consult Mr. Joshee, I must content myself with stating the opinion of Mrs. Carpenter and the Pundita Ramabai, and leave the text for the present unaltered.

In his memoranda of the last hours of his wife, Mr. Joshee mentions that the funeral services extended over thirteen days. It is customary after cremation in Hindustan to scatter the ashes of the deceased to the "four winds."

With some difficulty and against the wishes of his people, but doubtless with a strong desire to bear witness to Anandabai's devotion to this country, Gopal gathered the ashes of his wife together and they are now on their way to America. The box which contains them will be buried in the Eighmie lot in the Cemetery at Poughkeepsie, where a suitable stone will tell the short story of Anandabai's life.

In copying the letters in which Mrs. Joshee relates her dreams, or alludes to her early experiences, I have felt obliged to confine myself strictly to her own words, without attempting comment or explanation. May this little book — however weak and imperfect the picture which it presents — stimulate all hearts to noble charity, and convince whoever has hitherto doubted, that God never leaves any heart, whether heathen or civilized, without a possible witness to his Being and his Nature.

CAROLINE HEALEY DALL.

1603 "O" St., Washington, D. C.,
March, 1888.

A "MENTAL PHOTOGRAPH."

Written in Mrs. Carpenter's Album at Roselle, Sept. 3d, 1883, *by Anandabai Joshee.*

What is your favorite

1. Color? White.
2. Flower? The Rose.
3. Tree? The Mango.
4. Object in Nature? Mountains.
5. Hour? Sunrise and set.
6. Season? Spring.
7. Perfume? Jasmine.
8. Gem? Diamond.
9. Style of beauty? Perfection of form and manner.
10. Name, — male and female? Rama, Tara, Annie, Gopal, Vishnu, and Chrishna.
11. Painter? I love all.
12. Musician? Those who play on the violin and lyre.
13. Piece of architecture? The Taj Mahal.
14. Poet? Pope, Manu, and Kalidasa.
15. Poetess? Muktabai and Janabai.
16. Prose author? Goldsmith, Macaulay, Addison, Shastree Chiptoonka.
17. Character in History? Richard Cœur de Lion.
18. Book to take up for an hour? The Bhagavat-Gîtâ.

19.* What book, not a Bible, would you part with last? The History of the World.

20. What epoch would you prefer to live in? The Present.

21. Where would you prefer to live? In Roselle now, hereafter in Heaven.
22. What is your favorite amusement? Reading.
23.* What is your favorite occupation? Whatever is necessary to the common comfort.
24. What is your favorite trait of character? Sincerity.
25. What trait do you most detest? Dishonesty and infidelity.
26.* If not yourself, whom would you like to be? No one.
27.* What is your idea of happiness? Faith in God.
28.* What is your idea of misery? To follow one's own will.
29. What is your *bête noir?* Slavery and Dependence.
30. What is your ideal pleasure? To be rewarded for what I do.
31.* What is your distinguishing characteristic? I have not yet found out.
32. That of your husband? Benevolence.
33. What is the sublimest passion? Love.
34. What are the sweetest words? Love, charity, truth and hope.
35. What are the saddest? Lost, forsaken.
36. What is your aim? To be useful.
37. What is your motto? The Lord will provide.

* I have preserved this photograph in these pages mainly for the sake of directing attention to the remarkable answers to questions 19, 23, 26, 27, 28, and 31. These taken by themselves draw the picture plainly enough. Kalidasa mentioned in the answer to the 14th is the most famous of Indian dramatists — the author of Sacontala. I have not been able to find any account of Muktabai, Janabai, or Shastree Chiptoonka.

SYNOPSIS.

ANANDABAI JOSHEE, M. D.

Daughter of Gunputrao Amritaswar Joshee and Gungabai Joshee his wife.

Born in Poonah, India, March 31st, 1865. Child name, Yumna, popularly Jumna, or "Daughter of the Sun."

Married Gopal Vinayak Joshee, March 31st, 1874. Wife name Anandabai, or "Joy of my heart."

Sailed from Calcutta for New York, April 7th, 1883, being the first unconverted high-caste Hindu woman to leave her country.

Landed in New York, June 4th, 1883.

Graduated from the Woman's Medical College of Pennsylvania, March 11th, 1886, being the first Hindu woman to receive the degree of medicine in any country.

Appointed June 1st, 1886, to the post of Physician-in-charge of the Female Wards of the Albert Edward Hospital, Kolhapur, India.

Sailed from New York, Oct. 9th, 1886.

Died in Poonah, India, Feb. 26th, 1887.

CONTENTS.

Illustration.

LIFE OF ANANDABAI JOSHEE.

THE country which we call India, better known by the more familiar name of Hindustan, stretches from the Himmaleh Mountains to the Indian Ocean, and from the empire of Burmah to Afghanistan. It is eighteen hundred miles long, and fifteen hundred wide.

In the last half of the seventeenth century, under its great Mogul emperor Aurung-Zebe, Hindustan was divided into thirty-three provinces, which very nearly correspond to the thirty-three States recognized under the present British supremacy. To this great country, so divided, thirty-three different languages are popularly ascribed. These have a common foundation in the Sanscrit, but differ in their construction to such an extent that those who are native to the country are unwilling to call them dialects. Hindustanee, which is everywhere spoken, originated at the time of the Mahometan conquest, and was called by the Moguls Urdû Zabân, or "camp language."

It is a sort of *lingua franca*, and is used in all the provinces in addition to the local speech. In that part of the country called the Deccan, and in the south of Hindustan, six or eight languages are spoken, such as the Tamil and the Telingà, which are not supposed by Colebrooke or Campbell to have any foundation in the Sanscrit.

If the Hindus originally moved southward from central Asia bringing the Sanscrit with them, they found a native population south of the Ganges, and it is probable that the language of southern India represents that then spoken by the aborigines.

In the northwest of India, just south of the Punjaub and between Delhi and Scinde, is a country called Rajpootana. This country originally consisted of eight principalities, stretching over wide deserts and through mountain passes, nurturing a sturdy population able to endure cold and hunger, and standing in such a relation to the rest of Hindustan as the townsmen of Galilee once stood toward the people of Palestine. Until the British took possession of the country they were called "robbers and murderers." Yet in the town now called Rajapore, at the close of the fifteenth century, the great religious sect called the Sikhs was founded by Nanac Shah. The Sikhs worship one pure invisible God; they have a sacred scripture, which they keep in a small temple surrounded by the waters of the Golden Lotus. Their creed was intended by Nanac as a compromise between that of the Brahmins and that of Mahomet, and it is very singular that it should have taken root among the Rajpoots, because they, of all the peoples of the country, remained unconquered by the Moguls. The name "Sikhs" had been once confined to the Rajpoots, it means "lions," and had been given to them as the first military order among the Hindus. When religious persecution gave the followers of Nanac an opportunity to show their mettle, the name of "lions," or Sikhs, was transferred from their oppressors to themselves, and is still retained.

To speak properly of the history of the peoples or languages of Hindustan requires a profound scholarship, which I am far from claiming; but a few words concerning it were necessary before we could enter on the life of Anandabai Joshee. It must be understood clearly in advance that the Hindus are not one people, do not speak one language, and that the customs and history of one province are not the customs and history of any other. The Sikhs and the Rajpoots are well known by name to the students of the history of

British India, but their doings have been eclipsed during the last two centuries by the prowess of the Mahrattas. The origin of this people is wholly obscure to Europeans; but Anandabai asserted that they themselves possessed the records of two thousand years of independent existence. They are supposed to be an offshoot of the mountaineers of Rajpootan, driven south by stress of famine and war. They first became known to Europeans a little after the year 1300, but they were well established in the possession of the great city of Poonah at that time, and were carrying on destructive wars with other native States. The Mahrattas assert that they were never conquered by the Moguls.

There is nothing in the original Hindu scriptures to require the seclusion or subjection of women. The Hindus assert that this originated after the Mahometan conquest, in consequence of the licentious boldness of the Moslem soldiery; but there is evidence that it began to be practised as early as the eighth century. If this were so, the zenana probably originated in the brutalities of the early internecine contests, and was confirmed not more by the violence than the habits of the Mahometan conquerors. It would have been necessary to secure respect for women among the new-comers by secluding them, as they themselves secluded their own women. The name of Mahrattas was given to this people because, when they broke away from the original home of the Rajpoots, driven by war or famine or the Cossack's love of adventure, they settled in a district of Dowlatabad, to the south of Bombay, which was called Mharat.

In the early period of its history, the Mahratta people seem to have been governed in a feudal fashion. It was the custom of the reigning Rajah to reward his favorites for any service rendered, by large grants of land, or delegated sovereign powers. By degrees there grew up a nobility bearing the state of princes, sometimes independent of the Government, sometimes tributary to it, but for the most part true to its supremacy.

It was not until 1818, when the successive Rajahs of the Mahrattas had been in turn the prisoners of the successive ministers of State for more than a century, that, worn out by intestine divisions, the people asked the protection of the British Government, and surrendered a large part of the district of Poonah. Five hundred years ago the reigning Rajah, in a hot contest with a neighboring province, trusted the conduct of his forces to a young general of the Joshee family not yet twenty-one years of age. Success followed success, until his sovereign finally recalled him, to endow him with a palace in Poonah and a principality of sixty villages. He came back from the field to be received with flaming torches and gorgeous processions, and was allowed an hour's stay with his young wife. He knelt, kissed his sovereign's hand, departed, and lost his life in the next fray. He died before he was twenty-one, and left an only child, from whom Anandabai was descended. Her father was Gunputrao Amritaswar Joshee, her mother was Gungabai Durbagai Joshee; and as women do not take the names of their husbands in India, it is evident that the father and mother were descended from the same stem.

If I understand properly the record I took down from her lips, Anandabai was the sixth of ten children. Of her four brothers, two died before her. Of the five sisters, the first and fourth are dead.

There are still living her brothers,

Damodhar Ganesh-Joshee and

Vinayak Ganesh Joshee, as well as the three sisters,

Kasheebai Ganesh Joshee,

Waranusheebai Oomabai Onkar, and

Sundrabai Ganesh Joshee.

The steady insertion of the name of Ganesh doubtless bears some relation to the mother's family; and Waranusheebai, a sister older than the subject of our story, was married, and is a widow in easy circumstances.

At Poonah, in the Bombay Presidency, in the very palace that had been given by the Rajah to her victorious ancestor, there was born on the 31st of March, 1865, a little brown baby, whose future no one suspected. On the eleventh day she was called Yamuna, or Yumna, Daughter of the Sun, after the sacred river popularly called Jumna,—a name which she bore until her marriage. The little that we know of her childhood only piques our desire to know more. Her father is described by her cousin Ramabai as "a rich landholder of Kalyan, a town a little to the north of Bombay, where he was warmly regarded by the high caste people." The palace at Poonah was still in the possession of her grandparents and an uncle of her mother's, who was a distinguished Hindu physician.

It was to avail herself of this physician's services that Gungabai had gone to Poonah a short time before her daughter's birth. Yamuna grew up between Poonah and Kalyan. She was from the first a great pet of her father, and her happiest hours were passed upon his knee, under a great plane-tree in the Kalyan garden, where he went to rest every day after dinner. He owned many villages, and for the benefit of his servants and peasantry and after the manner of European landholders, he kept a chaplain. It was the duty of the priest who held this office to offer prayer and sacrifice, to instruct the people, and also to cleanse the shrines and images of the gods. Yamuna had never thought of the priest in a serious way, and was only four years old when she sat one day playing with her dolls and watching him as he washed the little images of jade, bitumen, or metal, and oiled them carefully before setting them back on their shrines. Suddenly it flashed into her mind that there was no difference between these images and her dolls. They did not move; they lay passive in the hand of the priest. They did not cry like children when he rubbed them hard, nor rejoice when he left them to themselves. Very eagerly she waited for her father to finish his dinner, and then seizing his hand ran away to the bench under the plane-tree.

"Papa," she exclaimed, hardly waiting to get her breath, "how can a god bear to have his face washed by a man?" And then, not waiting for any answer from the astonished Gunputrao, she went on to tell him what she had seen, and how the images lay in the priest's hand as if they had been her dolls.

"Those images are not gods," replied her father; "they are made to hold the thoughts of men to God while they pray. Some of them represent the love, and some the justice of God, and some only his creative power. My little daughter, can you pray to God without looking at any of those images?"

"Yes, indeed!" replied the child.

"Then you need never think of them again," was the reply; "they will be of no use to you."

"And I never did," continued his daughter, very simply, when she told the story.

The only other incident relating to this period of her life which is known to me has a truly Oriental flavor. Anandabai was neither a spiritualist nor a theosophist; but from her earliest childhood she dwelt apart, believed in a spiritual world which was even nearer to her than the world she touched, and held herself always ready to listen to "occult" voices and accept "occult" experiences.

There was in her home an immense genealogical record of the Joshees. It stretched over two thousand years, had been kept by the head of the family in each generation, and was illustrated by painted pictures of the costumes worn by its heroes, and the events briefly described on it. I imagine it was a roll. It was written on a sacred paper kept expressly for such uses, *from which no word could ever be effaced,* emulating in this respect the tablets of the recording angel. As it was always kept under lock and key, Anandabai thought that she had never seen it, and knew nothing about it, when she had the following dream. She had gone to bed as usual, at some time before she was five years old, when there suddenly appeared to her the figure of a young and handsome man, dressed in a manner, and carrying weapons, that she had never seen.

"Who are you?" she said, like any frightened child, when he fixed his eyes upon her.

"Do you not know who I am?" he said gravely.

"No."

"Go then to your father," resumed the soldier, "and tell him to make you acquainted with my life; for it is you who are to tread in my foosteps."

At this she waked, bathed in perspiration and trembling. In the morning she went to her father and earnestly entreated him to tell her about the "god" whom she had seen. Gunputrao was unable to identify the figure from Yamuna's description, but in the midst of many words, which I have forgotten, the soldier had said, —

"It is ungrateful to be ignorant of him whose blood flows in your veins."

From these words Gunputrao felt certain that it was one of his own ancestors who had appeared to his daughter, and he reverently opened his family roll. At last they came to a figure that Yamuna recognized at once as that of the man who had appeared to her. It was that of the young general who had founded the fortunes of her family, and in whose palace she had been born. From that time Gunputrao was even more tender toward his daughter; he not only gave her whatever she desired, but he paid special attention to her education.

The Mahrattas have never secluded their women; they walk the streets as securely and openly as those of Europe or America. Anandabai thought this was because they had never been exposed to the insolence of a Mogul conqueror; but perhaps it was also because the tribe began its existence in rough mountain passes, away from the "busy haunts of men."

It was when she was living a free life like that of a little country child in America, but with the character and intellectual development only possible to an American child of twice her age, that her first opportunity came to her. Gopal Vinyak Joshee was appointed a clerk in the Postal Department of Bombay in 1870, when Yamuna was only five years old. As he was a stranger in those parts, he eagerly sought the acquaintance of the head of his own family in that neighborhood. Gunputrao was an educated man. He had organized a school in one of the large rooms of the house in which he lived, and saw at once that Gopal's knowledge of Sanscrit would be of great advantage to Yamuna.

I never learned at what hours, or in what manner, Gopal taught; but Yamuna remained under his care for nearly three years, when Gopal was promoted to be post-master at Alibag, with an increase of salary, and at once prepared to leave the neighborhood. Yamuna's grief could not be repressed. "I thought I should never learn any more," she said; "and I would rather have died." Forgetting her love for father and mother, indifferent to brothers and sisters, she begged permission to go away with Gopal. Her father was sorely puzzled. Although only eight years of age, Yamuna was now marriageable.

It is not likely, from what followed, that her

mother approved of her studies, or her removal from her father's house; but the subservient position of a Hindu wife prevented her expressing any opinion. In this emergency, the grandmother from Poonah — the mother's mother — came to Yamuna's aid. "I will go with her," she said, "and I will shield her as if she were my own." She did go, and as long as she lived her grandchild was reverently grateful for the service.

I have not been able to ascertain the exact locality of Alibag; I suppose it was in the Bombay Presidency, and it must have been a small native town, as the salary Gopal received as postmaster was but little more than that given him as a clerk in Bombay. It was probably a Mahratta village not far from Kalyan, or the mother of Gungabai would hardly have been willing to go to it. At all events, when a third removal was made to Bhooj, the capital of Cutch, the grandmother returned home. From Alibag, Gopal had been transferred to Kolhapur, and it was probably there that the grandmother parted with the child, who was soon to be married to Gopal.

Yamuna was now older than most Hindu girls are when they marry, but she had never thought of marriage. Pursuing her studies with an eagerness that few women in any country could understand, all that she cared for was to remain with her teacher and continue her work. When therefore the marriage was proposed, no objection was made to it. Gopal was a widower, and he would have been scarcely human if he had not been touched by the devotion of his young pupil. He was an educated man, respected by his own people, and twenty years older than Yamuna. It is not likely that any charge had ever been brought against his character; for Gunputrao, who entered cheerfully into the arrangements for the wedding, was not a man to overlook that. Yamuna was married on the 31st of March, 1874, the day on which she completed her ninth year.

A Hindu woman can make no claim upon her father's estate. When she marries, the father agrees to give to her husband a certain sum, if he is rich and able, and he endows his daughter with such clothing, jewels, and utensils as he chooses. Yamuna was her father's favorite, and he had a trembling sense of the remarkable life she was to lead, based upon the dream which they had interpreted together. He gave her abundantly of his great wealth,—superb cashmeres, Dacca muslins bordered with gold, delicate jewels, bangles and anklets of solid gold, and ornaments that were heirlooms and would ordinarily have gone to a son. Still another thing showed his high trust in her: she was allowed to carry away from her home some of the most valued and sacred of the household gods, and the relics connected with them.

In an official statement made lately at Poonah, Gopal gives me the dates for this portion of my story, but he does not give the exact date of his removal to Bhooj, the capital of the province of Cutch. I am constrained to think it occurred in the spring of 1874, from the circumstances. Yamuna must have gone home to be married; and although her grandmother might well hesitate to go with her several hundred miles to the northwest, to an unknown and undesirable location like that of Cutch, there was no apparent reason why she should not remain at Kolhapur. As Cutch was within the Bombay Presidency, Gopal was undoubtedly obliged to report at Bombay, in removing from Kolhapur to Cutch, and either Poonah or Kalyan could be taken in the direct route to his new home.

Four days after her marriage, in conformity to the custom of the Mahrattas, and the more completely to affiliate her to her husband's family, Yamuna dropped the name by which her father's loving lips had called her, and assumed that of

Anandabai, or "Joy of my Heart," by which she was afterward known. Up to this time she had suffered no peculiar hardships. Her husband was poor, but his salary was equal to their modest wants. The proposal of marriage, according to the custom of the country, came from the wife's family; and the father of Anandabai could not have been ignorant of the character of the province to which his child was now going. He believed that this young daughter was to follow in the footsteps of her great ancestor so far as to shed a fresh lustre on the name of her family. The sacredness attached to her vision spurred him to aid her in every way that he could. At this moment he could hardly be expected to see how her removal to a distant and demoralized province could develop her destiny.

The "island" of Cutch must be nearly four hundred miles to the northwest of Kalyan or Bombay. Surrounded on three sides by water, and bounded on the other by an immense salt-marsh produced by the earthquake of 1819, Cutch is an island only during the rainy season. This marsh, or "runn," one hundred and fifty miles long by sixty wide, furnishes a hiding-place for criminals and bandits. The country produces cotton, gum, and nuts, which are sent in native vessels to Africa, three thousand miles away, where they are exchanged for ivory and hides, and to Guzerat, where the mariners exchange cotton for grain. Twenty years before Gopal and Anandabai went to Bhooj, the town is described as consisting of low, mean dwellings, so crowned by white mosques and temples, shaded by date-trees, as to present a picturesque appearance at a distance. It is a fortified town, standing half-way up a hill. The people are of Rajpoot descent, but more than half the population profess a sort of spurious Mahometanism, adhering to many Hindu observances. This is especially true of the Jharejah tribe, to which the reigning prince belongs. Neither its morals nor its manners bear out the boast of virtuous simplicity Gopal was so fond of making. It had a population of twelve thousand adults at the time of which I speak, and the universal practice of female infanticide had reduced the number of native women to thirty! The people were then ignorant, indolent, and drunken, and obliged, of course, to procure their wives from other tribes. The Reports to the House of Commons show a terrible local demoralization.

Anandabai did not like her neighbors; and I think it must have been here, in her tenth year, that she began to do her own cooking, cleaning her brass vessels, and tossing up her pastry in hands like those of a Greek model. Hard work she had never known. It began here with the necessity of repression, some regard to the proprieties of womanhood, and a desire to escape from the influences around her. She never complained either then or afterward of anything in her lot; but she said, "I was never at home there." It was a religious ceremony, making marriage irrevocable, which she had entered into in the spring of 1874.

When the second ceremony, consummating the marriage, took place, I do not know; but Anandabai's only child was born in her fourteenth year, probably at Kolhapur, some time early in 1878, as Gopal wrote from that town in 1878 and 1879. It lived about ten days, and died, as Anandabai thought, because it did not have a competent physician. It was this that first led her to think of studying medicine. "A child's death does no harm to its father," she once said, "but its mother does not want it to die."

In all the thoughts and schemes that grew out of her bereavement her husband seems to have shared; and those who heard him speak in this country will hardly understand the letter addressed to one of the Presbyterian missionaries from Kolhapur on the 4th of September, 1878. It is probable that he had come into contact with the missionaries in every town in which he had lived. He kept a steady eye to the advantages to be gained by Anandabai's thorough education, and perhaps he was not perfectly frank when he wished to gain their co-operation. When his wife's proud heart took fire at certain indignities, it was he who urged her to go back to the school in Bombay. At all events, his learning and intelligence won a certain hearing for this letter. It was forwarded to the "Missionary Review" published at Princeton, and printed in January, 1879. Gopal expresses a warm interest in female education, and says that he should be glad to live in America if his wife could study there. The letter was supported by one of the local missionaries in terms which showed that he based this support on what he thought a rational expectation of Gopal's conversion.

Dr. Wilder, the editor of the "Review," seems to have published these letters chiefly for the purpose of printing his own reply, written Oct. 14, 1878. In this letter he thoroughly discourages Gopal's project. He evidently does not wish any unconverted Hindu to come to America; he believes that his intelligent correspondent will be led to "confess Christ," and trusts to the mission schools to educate Mrs. Joshee sufficiently. Little did he think that this very letter would be the means of bringing her to this country. At various times it has aroused the indignation of Anandabaï's friends; but from a somewhat wide experience of male Hindus, I cannot consider their visits to the West profitable to others or themselves. With the single exception of the author of "The Oriental Christ," I have seen no Hindu who seemed to me prepared intellectually and morally for the freedom he would find in American society; nor are Americans prepared for the air of innocence and exaltation worn by very undeserving Orientals. I have no doubt that Dr. Wilder honestly shrank from the possibilities; and I differ from him only in this: I do not think any "conversion" works a miracle in a man's intellectual status; and I do not think Gopal, if he had "confessed Christ," would have been one bit better able to understand his environment in America than he proved himself while walking in the shadows of the old Vedas. It is not learning, intellect, subtlety, or imagination that is wanting in the average Hindu; it is purity, faith, and honesty.

So felt I before I had seen this Hindu woman, and now I pity every one who was not privileged to see and know her.

Let us see what became of Dr. Wilder's letter.

Early in the spring of 1880 a lady almost as remarkable in philanthropy and spirituality as Anandabai herself, went from the little town of Roselle, in New Jersey, to see her dentist in Elizabeth. Upon the dentist's table, among other interesting things, lay the old number of the "Missionary Review," and she took it up to wile away the moments of waiting. She knew nothing of Hindustan or its people. Gopal's letter seemed to her a genuine cry for help, and her whole soul was roused to indignation by the brutal manner in which she thought this cry was repulsed. In the tumult of her mind she copied the address, and then as she went slowly home she remembered that she knew nothing of British India, nothing of possible ways or means, and she put the whole subject out of her mind. The next morning it returned; she could not get rid of the impression that it belonged to her to answer that letter.

Early in March, 1880, Mrs. Carpenter wrote to Gopal, using the Kolhapur address; but after the migratory fashion of the British office, the postmaster had meanwhile left that town for Bombay, and was now among the dreary hills of Bhooj. In this letter she offered the shelter of her own home to the young wife in whom she had already begun to feel a tender interest. It was some months before she received a reply, which led directly to the freest correspondence with Anandabai. The strength and sweetness of Mrs. Carpenter's letters seem to have won Anandabai's confidence at once. In a very little while she had adopted Mrs. Carpenter into her family, called her her aunt, and wrote of the children at Roselle as her cousins.

"Then began for me," writes Mrs. Carpenter, "a regular course of education in Hindu manners, customs, religious rites, and everything of interest which her ready pen and remarkable mastery of English could set forth, while I in return answered all her queries. Newspapers, magazines, pictures, flowers, and seeds were exchanged. The exchange of photographs was most interesting to me, because of the peculiar style of dress. How strange seemed the bare arms with many bracelets, the bare space under one arm, the bare feet with their anklets and toe-rings, and the mark on the forehead! That I should be corresponding with a young woman dressed like this who could write elegant English seemed past belief. I was puzzled by a blemish on the upper lip; and in response to my inquiries, Anandabai wrote: 'It is the nose-ring that you see in my photograph, between my nose and my lip. It consists of one gold wire, upon which are fastened pearls, some pendent and others fixed and star-shaped. We are fond of many ornaments. Our hands, feet, necks, and waists are all adorned "to the teeth." Even our noses and ears are bored in many places to hold them. Holes are bored through the lower part of the left nostril for the nose-ring, and all around the edge of the ear for jewels. This may appear barbarous to the foreign eye; to us it is a beauty! Everything changes with the clime. The Mahratta dresses and ornaments are quite different from those in use in other parts of India.' We exchanged locks of hair, although Anandabai said it was not the custom of her people; only widows were allowed to cut their hair."

In writing of widows at another time, she said to Mrs. Carpenter:—

"To tell you the truth, I shudder at the very sound of the word. Your American widows may have difficulties and inconveniences to struggle with, but weighed in the scale against ours, all of them put together are but as a particle against a mountain. When we began to write, I cared little for letters; but I now see how the daily occurrences of life, which I thought so trifling, may yield instruction."

Later she continued:—

"I wish to preserve my manners and customs, unless they are detrimental to my health. Can I live in your country as if I were in my own, and what will it cost me? When I think over the sufferings of women in India in all ages, I am impatient to see the Western light dawn as the harbinger of emancipation. I am not able to say what I think, but no man or woman should depend upon another for maintenance and necessaries. Family discord and social degradation will never end till each depends upon herself."

At this time, not being very well, Anandabai went to Kalyan. From this town she sent some silver filigree from Cutch to her friends; and later she continues:—

"We reached Calcutta on the 4th of April, 1881. The flowers I sent you from Cutch were wild flowers. I had made a garden in my compound there, but I had no liking for the care of it, and I owe you a great debt for urging me to undertake it."

And she goes on to tell how flowers are used in the Hindu religious services, how each god is supposed to have his favorite flowers, trees, and plants, and speaks of their specific virtues.

In May she wrote very despondently of her

own health, and of coming to America, and goes on: —

"We have met with so many misfortunes that I do not think my husband will continue long in the service. We have no friends here. Our diet, manners, and customs are different from those of the Bengalis; nor can we ask sympathy from the English. We live in the house of a German milliner. When I came, all the servants gathered round to have a look at me, and the lady peeped through her window and laughed. If we read to each other, she begs us to stop because her children cannot go to sleep. She told some people that we quarrelled all night, and asserted that I was not a married woman. For a fortnight we could not get enough to eat, although our pockets were full. Our 'kit,' containing baggage, bedding, and clothing, remained behind, and we had to sleep on mats. The ground was damp. Such a thing had never happened to us before. You see how hard it is to travel where we have no friends. What would happen to us in your country?

"Our great Raja Harischandra was persecuted like the Job of your Bible. He was deprived of his all, of his wife and child, but he did not break his vow. When he stood the test, God restored all to him."

Hope still cheered Anandabai, although her husband seems wholly to have lost courage. In June, 1881, she writes: —

"Calcutta is trying to the utmost. Physically we are reduced in health and strength. The climate is very warm. It has begun to rain, and yet the heat is not less. We go out for a walk, and the Europeans talk and laugh when they see us. The natives stand still, and order their carriages to stop, while they stare at us. They can never be persuaded that we are married. There is so much of the zenana system here that a woman can scarcely stand in the presence of her relatives, — much less before her husband. Her face is always veiled. She is not allowed to speak to any man, — much less to laugh with him. Even the Baboos, who have spent years in England, will not drive here, with their wives, in open carriages. If it is so with the educated people, how much more prejudiced must be the illiterate! One Sepoy insulted us when we were walking on the Esplanade. He asked my husband who the woman was that he had with him. My husband was angry, and asked his name, to report him to the commissioner. This brought him to his senses, and he went away courteously."

The first entire letter which I select from her correspondence is dated —

CALCUTTA, Aug. 27th, 1881.

MY DEAR AUNT, — In my last I acknowledged your letter of July 3d. I beg to answer it now. I have no more of your letters to answer, and hope not to be in arrears in future. Your letter, that I am about to reply to, is so consoling and heart-soothing that it is most welcome. We are not yet free from troubles. During the last five months anxieties have arisen without and within. We were about to forget them, when another serious mishap occurred.

A special despatch from the Viceroy to the Governor of Bengal was due here on Sunday, the 14th. It was watched by special officers from Simla. It was received by my husband on passing a receipt. It was to be immediately sent to the Governor's camp. My husband was therefore going to the railway with one of his assistants, into whose hand the important letter was given. As they were running fast, to get into a hackneyed carriage that could be met on the road, the letter dropped down. A searching inquiry was made all along, but in vain. The letter disappeared in the twinkling of an eye. The consternation and stir it must have given rise to throughout the town will be better conceived than described. All the high officials held councils. The police were sent in all directions. The persons of the men on the road were examined. Not a stone was left unturned. My husband and his assistants were in custody; depositions were made, — in short, it was a day which will never be forgotten. My husband was suspended, pending orders from Government.

You may imagine what state of mind I was in, and how engrossed must have been my heart by grief!

We gave up all hopes of service, and were preparing to start for any place. We first determined to go to Rangoon, in Birmah, and stay there for a time. It was my intention to make an address before the English-speaking people there, and thus obtain pecuniary assistance to leave for another place. From there we were thinking of going to Hong-Kong, and thence to Japan, and from Japan to America. This project may appear very wild to an outsider, but it was a necessity. We could not retrace our steps to Bombay, nor was it easy to travel in Bengal or the Punjaub, where the zenana is rampant. But, thanks to Providence, my husband has been reinstated! My husband never lost anything before but in Calcutta; he had never seen police court before but in Calcutta; we had never had scandals in our neighborhood but in Calcutta; we had never seen double-tongued men before but in Calcutta. I do not know how much misery is still in store for us. I have been telling him to sever his connection with Government to avoid any future calamities; but he is wavering. He thinks it very difficult to earn a livelihood; but I think otherwise. Whether he is more experienced, and knows the world better, and therefore cannot do anything hastily, or whether the more a man is advanced in position, and the more he gets beyond what is actually necessary to sustain life, the more susceptible of imaginary difficulties he becomes, I do not know; but in my opinion man must fear nothing but God. As God is over us and supplies our wants, I do not know why we should have a thought for the morrow. Man wants but little, and for that little he bears a world of care, which I do not understand. Let me be here, or in any part of the globe, I will get my bread.

But to return to your letter. Had there been no difficulties and no thorns in the way, the man would have been in his primitive state and no progress made in civilisation and mental culture. Your letter is a sermon which we needed. Each line is full of meaning and world wide knowledge. I do not know how many times I should thank you.

We have our food cooked by ourselves. We do not get these things ready in the Bazaar. As we had no pots in which to cook, we could not do otherwise than go without, till we had our own furniture brought home. We never employ low caste people to attend to household affairs, and as we were but two, in a place where servants and other things available were of no use to us we could but remain fasting. Imagine, you go to a place where there are no shops and you have plenty of money in your pocket. There is nobody to give you food, what will you do with your money? I have told you before, that as the people of India are not a travelling class, there are no hotels for us at each halting place. When we go on a travel we generally take with us articles of food, prepared in milk and sugar, without a drop of water.

Any thing prepared in water is not carried and eaten. If eaten it must be prepared then and there and eaten on the spot. So money is not always a useful article in India. I know a gentleman who was travelling in "Kandesh." He was not admitted to house or temple so he had to pass the night under a tree. Next morning he went from door to door, but could get no one to cook for him, though he was willing to pay for it enormously. At night he got hold of an old lady, who agreed to serve him, provided he would tell nobody.

I have dreams about my departed friends, but never feel their presence when I am awakened. I often dream of going to America and holding long conversations. What does it portend?

I enclose a letter for Eighmee. I hope she will write to me again. Her hand is after your fashion.

affectionately yours,

ANANDABAI JOSHEE.

Several things are remarkable in this letter. Those who saw Anandabai and her husband together in this country cannot fail to recognize in her description of the trouble at the Post Office the restless excitable nature of the man and the sweet serenity of the woman. Those projects of hurried travel were all his, but she does not disown them. We smile tenderly over the expressive epithet of "hackneyed" as applied to a public carriage, but Anandabai could not know that it was the abuse of the public coach which had caused this word to stand for all common-place and tiresome things. Its history is a curious example of the growth of language. Originally applied, as Richardson shows, to an active noisy horse or ney, which vented its activity in frequent neighs, and as such horses were most frequently found attached to public carriages, the word hack-ney was soon transferred to the carriage itself, and when the dusty vehicle began to have a fixed character in the public mind, the substantive soon came to do duty as an adjective for all manner of things.

In this letter Anandabai expresses the great annoyance she felt, at the observation she attracted in Bengal. "The zenana is rampant" she says. Once when I was trying to protect her from unpleasant observation in the City of Philadelphia, she thanked me by saying, "I am more at home here than I was in Calcutta." She is only sixteen, yet she wonders at the world of care people are willing to carry to acquire goods that are by no means necessary! Do we not find a touch of the "Oriental Christ" in the words "As God is over us, and supplies our wants, I do not know why we should have a thought for the morrow?" She could not speak English at this time, although she wrote it so easily. The letter closes with an allusion to the impulse which had prompted Mrs. Carpenter to write to her. Her father Gunputrao Joshee, had now been dead for some time, and she fancied from something that Mrs. Carpenter had written, that her new friend had been under his influence. If he had lived the family opposition which made her life and duty so very hard would have been averted.

She now began to study Sanscrit in earnest that she might be able to show English scholars "the sublimity of the Shasters."

In a letter written about this time, she says, "Any thing which cannot be enjoyed by the whole world is bad for me!" Was there ever a more pronounced socialism? Her life in Calcutta had brought her new and varied trials, which she felt more sharply than any in the morasses of "Cutch." We know from this letter that she was very poorly fed. Her landlady did nothing to help her out of her trouble. When she went into the street or to the Bazaar she was followed and pelted. "This country is not a good one for us for we are living in a manner not warranted by its customs," she wrote. Feeling the dejection consequent on starvation she says, "I think I shall not live long. To live and be useful is of the grace of God, but to die is the direct proof of his grace; still to die before the call of nature is the desertion of duty." Wonderful thoughts these to be stirring in that young brain. To one who knows anything of the sanitary condition of the smaller towns of India, it is impossible to contemplate with patience the several changes in her career. Daintily fresh always was everything about her that she could control, but at Barrackpore, from which she writes in December, she again alludes to fever and headache. She had not been well for more than a year. From Nov. 1880, to March, 1881, she had been constantly ailing. In Sept. and October, 1881, she was so unwell as to be carried to a friend's house to be nursed. It was after hearing of this illness, that a friend of Mrs. Carpenter's, a lady who had no special interest in Anandabai, received a prescription in her sleep which was sent to her. I give it exactly as it was transmitted.

1 ounce of black Cohosh,
½ an ounce of Juniper berries,
1 ounce of Virginia snakeroot,
½ ounce of Buchu leaves.

Put this in four quarts of water and boil it down to one quart. Add one pint of the best Holland gin, and take half a wine glass after breakfast and just before going to bed. Begin with a little smaller dose, and repeat the prescription twice.

This would not be worth relating if it were not for the consequences. Anandabai took the medicine in December of 1881, and it is not till October, 1883, that we find again in her letters the pitiful words, "I am not very well," words which had been written in every letter previously received and which we came to understand later as having very serious meaning.

This is what she herself says about it, writing from

BARRACKPORE, BENGAL, Dec. 26th, 1881.

MY DEAR FRIEND, Your favor of Oct. 10th. came too late for a reply in last month. I am much better now, at least, free from fever. I am however thinking of taking the medicine, which you so kindly sent as prescribed for me by your good Doctor. I am now more independent and able to have things to my satisfaction. To tell you the truth, I always labor under inward impressions. I solve many difficult things while sleeping. I was not able to cut different kinds of native dresses for men and women, but I have learnt how in dreams. While sleeping, I dreamed that I had cut such and such shapes and sewed them. Next morning I when awakened actually did the same and according to memory and found everything fit and complete. Whenever I have to learn anything by heart, I do it when asleep. In the day, I read the passage to be committed to memory but once, and in sleep I read it over and over and repeat it next morning, without a mistake. Whenever I find any difficult passage in poetry I pass it over in the day, but in sleep I paraphrase it correctly and the next morning I am all right in translating it. I do not know who teaches me, but I learn in this way. I am therefore strongly inclined to believe that this medicine, prescribed in sleep will help me.[1]

As I am not familiar with the English or American houses, I do not know how to satisfy your curiosity about the city house. We were living in a house, like those in which Europeans live in India.

I shall however try to give you a description of a native dwelling in Bengal, in my next letter, as I once described to you our dwelling in Bombay.

The death of your good President has been mourned all over India. Every native paper had a leading article as if the loss was our own. This is an example

[1] "I have myself not infrequently got out of bed at night to write a thought or sentiment that had occurred to me in a semi dozing condition. A dream has some times served to solve an intricate mathematical problem, one that could not be solved in the waking state by the most powerful efforts of the mind." *Autobiography of Dr. S. D. Gross*, Vol. I. p. 178.

of how good men live and die. They live for the public good and die in service. Thanks for the pamphlets of Shaker. They are Christian in principle.

As you are not born and brought up in Hindu religion you will not, I am afraid, appreciate its true merits. No religion is bad, but its followers and selfish interpreters. Our priests are prejudiced and corrupt as are those of other religions. I dislike them as a class. I would rather be ignorant and illiterate than to have partial knowledge of every thing. As you value sickness as a means for the enjoyment of happiness, so I regard irreligious people as pioneers. If there had been no priesthood this world would have advanced ten thousand times better than it has now. So you need not expect to learn anything from our priests, who are no doubt groping in darkness. Spiritual truths which lighten all burdens, and call for no sacrifices, are our teachers. Our forefathers used to commune with the All pervading Force, and derived knowledge therefrom. They disregarded external duties and put too much stress on the acquirement of self knowledge for the emancipation of the soul.

I am sorry I forgot all about the wedding of the Bengali Babu though I promised to give you some account of it. The services of the occasion were formalities like the Christian. The parties were united by mutual promises made before a magistrate. The marriage was registered before the ceremonies were formally performed by a Bengali minister. This is copying English fashion. I do not understand why this is given precedence to the old customs which were more established.

I am glad to inform you, that if I have at all received any schooling, it was for a year only, when we were in Bombay. The lady superintendent was Miss Robson, who was very much interested in my education. She belongs to the Mission established by the Society for the Propagation of the Gospel. I love these Mission ladies for their enthusiasm and energy, but I dislike blindness to the feelings of others. This lady compelled me to read the Bible on pain of expulsion from the school. I told her I would not, and came home. I informed my husband, and said I did not want to go to that school again. But he expostulated with my rashness. He said that we would not lose anything by reading the Bible, and brought me round, to going to School, where I then abided by the rules. As a whole, I have nothing to say against the Bible, which is a code of moral rules, except the assertion, "He that believeth shall be saved," and "he who believeth not shall be damned." I have all along found the Missionaries very headstrong, and contemptuous of the faiths of others. How arbitrary would it be if I were to say that all you believed was nonsense, and all I believed was just and proper! My dear friend, I have nothing to despise. The whole universe is a lesson to me. I am required by duty to respect every creed and sect, and value its religion. I therefore read the Bible with as much interest as I read my own religious books. I sincerely thank you for your undivided sympathies with me and my husband in the sudden fall into the depth of anxiety and distress brought about by that sad event.

If I had been called to share the storms with my husband, I would have done nothing but my duty which I owe him as his deserving wife. There would have been nothing commendable or heroic in it. Let there be any amount of difficulties or distresses, and I think I shall be more than equal to face them. My hearty love to Eighmee and Helena.

Affectionately yours,

ANANDABAI JOSHEE.

In spite of a certain crudeness of expression there is a wonderful maturity of thought in this letter. I think no one can read without emotion the paragraph beginning, "I have nothing to despise, the whole universe is a lesson to me."

The next letter is written from Serampore. Barrackpore and Serampore are two small towns about ten miles north of Calcutta on the two opposite banks of the Hooghly. Each is reported to contain from twelve to fifteen thousand inhabitants but they are very different in character.

Barrackpore has been the country seat of the Governor Generals for more than forty years. It has fine residences, a beautiful park and a large military cantonment. Serampore is now a Hindu village. It is neatly built, in European fashion, stretching along the banks of the river for a mile. It was long the headquarters of the Protestant Missions and was ceded by Denmark to Great Britain in 1845. That Mr. Joshee should have been successively removed from an important position in Calcutta to the offices in these small towns would seem to indicate some dissatisfaction on the part of the government, occasioned perhaps by the lost letter, but there were no more changes. At Serampore, Anandabai remained until she started for America. From her copious letters to Mrs. Carpenter I select the following.

SERAMPORE, April 18th, 1882.

As intimated in my last, we left Barrackpore on the first, and arrived here the same evening. The river is only a mile wide, and we crossed in boats. Serampore is an old town of historical note. The first Missionary College in India was established here. It is still flourishing. There are many rich landholders, whose houses are princely. But the inhabitants are as barbarous and superstitious as they were hundreds of years ago. If the men are friendly they will not allow their women to associate with their own sex, if they are foreigners like me. I can form no acquaintance with them, unless I were to become a Missionary and force my way into the Zenana. You must not suppose they would not like to see the world, and yet some of the Bengali women who have been educated follow very barbarous customs. It is customary among us to eat "Vida" compounded of thirteen ingredients, namely betel leaves, betel nut, chunam, almond, camphor, saffron, cloves, cardamon, and so on. This "Vida" stains the teeth, tongue and mouth a red color. Some of these Bengalis stain the outside of their lips and so expose themselves to contempt.

I rely on God, and do not seek to know who are his individual messengers to me. Take any religion you like and you will find that its founder was a holy man. Go to his followers and you will find holy men the exception. I am glad to inform you that Miss Robson's school has been closed owing to her obstinacy. Soon after I left, she required all her scholars to read the Bible, and the result was that her pupils, ninety in number, left her, and she went home never to return.

In January, 1882, Anandabai sent out her gift of the Tila seed comfits, the making of which she describes in the following letter. She asked that they might be distributed among her friends according to the Hindu custom at the New Year, with the words

"Accept these Tila seeds, and be friendly with me throughout the year."

The Tila seeds are of three kinds, the white, red and black. I think it was the black which Anandabai used for her comfits. An oil is extracted from all of them, and is now exported to France, where it serves to adulterate olive oil.

SERAMPORE, BENGAL, May 16th, 1882.

MY DEAR FRIEND, — Your favors of March and April are with me for reply. At the head of each letter are beautiful pictures which are really worth looking at. I am glad to hear that the Tila seeds have at last reached you. I have requested you to eat them up, as they are intended for that. The way they are prepared is not difficult to learn, but I do not know enough to describe it. Take one pound of sugar and as much water and boil it till it becomes a little thick, so that if dropped on the ground it will look like a pearl and will run if you blow it, yet will not be hardened or dried into a pill. This sugar juice should be kept in a pot. Then the seeds should be wet, their skins removed, and again dried: put a brass pan over a light fire, and shake the seeds in it till they are swollen. Then move them to and fro with your fingers, and put five drops of the sugar on them at a time, shaking them till all are coated. Then you will have Tilas like mine. I am very much interested in the work you do from morning till evening. You will find the women of this country, both rich and poor, employing their time as usefully as you do. I am glad our household business perfectly resembles yours, but alas! how few there are among the European residents of India who follow in the footsteps of their forefathers.

My time is not so usefully employed as yours, but I will give you an account of the life which the generality of our women lead. We get up at five o'clock. We first answer the calls of nature, which is the primary duty, without which no person is clean to do any business, much less to worship God and prepare food. We sweep the ground, and wash all the copper and brass pots used for drinking purposes and worship. Then we oil and comb and dress our hair with several kinds of ornaments. Then, if there be children in the house, rice is prepared for them at about half past seven. Children eat it with salt and ghee. *Ghee* is boiled butter. Milk is sometimes used with rice. Children use pickles and "Papad" made of kidney beans, pounded with seasoning, such as cummin, pepper, chili, salt, and sometimes fennel. We begin to give rice to children when they are one year old. Hand-made breads of wheat flour are sometimes made for children's breakfast. After this is done we are engaged in putting all articles to rights before we sit down to cook them. As soon as vegetables are brought from the market, we wash them and then cut them into small pieces. So are rice, pulse and wheat flour cleaned and kept ready for cooking. We usually prepare five or six vegetables, and an equal number of other sour, hot, and sweet articles called "Koshimbiris." Plantains, guavas, and other fruits are cut and filled with spices.

Our stove is earthen, by the side of which we sit to cook after bathing and changing our night clothes and putting on sacred garments, which have been washed, and dried in a room where no one could go to touch them.

First we put an iron pan or a brass pot on the stove and put a little oil in that. When it is hot, rye seeds and cummin are thrown into it. When they are properly fried and broken, we put the vegetables in and cook them without water. We take our meals twice a day. The first meal about noon, the second from seven to eight in the evening. As a rule men take their meals before the women who serve them. A married woman does not eat until she has served her husband. After dinner, the men go to bed, and women are engaged in removing and washing the dishes, and cow-dunging the earthen floors, after which we change our clothes, and sit down, preparing for next day's cooking, cleaning rice and so on. We cut and sew our clothes till half-past five. We then go to the temple and return home after six o'clock, when we are again employed in preparing articles for supper. This occupies us until nine, when we prepare our beds and sleep. This is what women in India generally do. They have no letters to write, or books to read. They do not receive or make calls, except among their own female relatives. They do not speak with men, even with their own husbands, in presence of somebody.

I hope Helena has begun to attend school. It is getting very warm here, and much sickness prevails. My husband has been unwell. He has applied for one year's furlough. If he gets it, we shall start for America. It was our intention to secure a passage for Japan, and thence to America, but it is a circuitous route and expensive, so we intend going through England. Can you tell me how many days it will take, and what is the fare? I suppose Roselle is not far from New York.

I have much pleasure to inform you that I had some Bengali ladies invited to my house one evening and I was very much astonished to see them bow down before me, as if I were God! They were peculiarly interested in my dress and ornaments. They said the Maharastras had a respectable dress of their own, while Bengalis are half naked. I began this letter on the 16th, but was abruptly invited to Calcutta by my kind lady for a party which she gave in honor of her son's thread ceremony.

Your affectionate niece,

ANANDABAI JOSHEE.

This quaint account of the manufacture of the comfits sent by Anandabai, as a new Year's greeting, lets us into some of the secrets of Hindu cooking. From the time that she first began to write to Mrs. Carpenter, to that of her own arrival in this country, the little Hindu girl sent by mail or ship all sorts of curious things to illustrate the dress, food and customs of her country. *Hers* was no bric-a-brac collection. Scarce an article in it had any claim to prettiness, but the thoroughness with which she managed to exhibit Oriental life would have done credit to a Centennial Commissioner. Samples of all sorts, millet, buckwheat, pease and beans, were brought in small phials. All herbs, roots, seeds, and gums used in medicine were put up in the same fashion. Then followed the cooking utensils made of brass or pottery, the furnaces or chafing-dishes of coarse earthenware, the family idols and their shrines, and last of all, the letters which carefully described each.

This "Tila" is the *Sesamum orientale*, always connected in the Oriental mind with the occult forces, and carrying a hidden meaning as it is sent from one friend to another. The "Open Sesame" of the Arabian Nights is an invocation to the secret creative forces hidden in this tiny germ and permitted to work elsewhere.

"Ghee," she tells us, is "boiled butter," but why should butter be boiled? Because, otherwise, it could not be used at all, in many parts of India. Butter must there be made from milk, often by simply shaking it in a bottle, for it is impossible to let the milk stand until the cream rises. After the butter is made, it is scalded, clarified and so carried to market, otherwise it would be rancid in twenty-four hours. This is "Ghee," and in it all Hindu vegetables are cooked.

Many vegetables are used in India, which seem to us as innutritious as the "fried grass" of which Daniel Webster once partook at a rural neighbor's. Buckwheat is roasted, and eaten in the grain and tender buckwheat leaves are stewed in "ghee" like beans or pulse.

The practice of "*cow-dunging*" the floors of apartments does not seem very pleasant, it is therefore necessary to explain it. When Mr. Dall first went to Calcutta, he found the Hindus everywhere sweeping their houses and compounds with brooms made of twigs. Of course, it could not be thoroughly done, and one of the first articles manufactured in the Useful Arts School was the European broom, the handles, the broom corn, and the finished articles being several times sent out from Boston. After the earthen floor of a native house is swept, it is sprinkled with water in which cow-dung has been dissolved.

This water stands until it is clear, and is really a solution of ammonia. The effect of it upon the earthen floors is to purify and harden them. It must be remembered that the Hindus consider everything relating to the cow as sacred, and primitive experience probably pointed out the usefulness of this application.

The allusion to the "bowing down" of the Bengali ladies may puzzle those who are unacquainted with Hindu life.

The Mahrattas, among whom Anandabai had been bred, greet each other with dignity much like Europeans. The Bengalis prostrate themselves, and this astonished Anandabai as much as it would one of us.

The next letter from Serampore contains a touching Hindu story, and an interesting account of the "imposition of the thread," which may be considered as the consecration of the adult Brahmin according to the Shasters.

Those who read between the lines can easily see what the story of Savitri had become to Anandabai.

SERAMPORE, BENGAL, June 17th, 1881.

MY DEAR FRIEND, I now pick up my pen to write as I promised. To-day is the day of mailing, and I suspect I shall not be able to post in time. I am sorry to inform you, that our starting for America has been postponed for about six months, as a furlough cannot be had before.

I will send the price of the three books you so kindly sent me two years ago, through the money order system which will begin on the first of July.

I now turn to your question, "What is the *thread* ceremony?" I will try to quench your thirst of curiosity. There are sixteen such ceremonies among us, from birth to death. "Thread ceremony" is the eighth in order. It is initiating a Brahmin boy of eight years in spiritual knowledge. After this, the boy must live at his preceptor's house, and study Vedas and many other things till he is twenty years of age. And if during twelve years he is very well educated, he is then allowed to come to his father's house, but if not, he is not allowed till he finishes his study. He must pass this time, which is devoted to knowledge, in celibacy and then his marriage takes place. He should pass twenty or twenty-five years in the company of his family, until he is forty or forty-five years of age. The remainder of his life should pass in solitude until death put a stop to it. In this ceremony Brahmins are fed, money is given to the poor, and a *triple thread*, prepared at home, is taken in hand and made holy by repeating Vedic verses. This is afterward worn by the boy round his neck and under his right hand as a garland. I will send you an Almanac from which you may see how it is worn. Then the boy becomes a holy Brahmin. Before this ceremony he is allowed to dine with his parents, that is to say, they can eat from one dish, but when he has passed it and becomes what is called a "Munjàh," he must eat alone by himself. This ceremony is performed by three castes, the Brahmin, the Kshatriya. and the Vaishya. Among Brahmins in the eighth year, among Kshatriyas in the eleventh, and among Vaishyas in the twelfth. After the ceremony, the boy must perform certain religious austerities twice a day. This ceremony corresponds to baptism among Christians. It was good in principle, but now-a-days it is a mere ceremonial. Parents now spend thousands of rupees to gratify their vanity and do no good to the boy, who is fed at home, instead of being allowed to stay with his preceptor and live by begging, which is the principal injunction of our Shastras. A Munjàh has no right to eat at his father's. I am afraid I have not done justice to the subject, but will try to write more fully before long.

We had a holiday on the first, which is called "Walasavitri." Wala means a banyan tree, and Savitri was the obedient wife of a man named Satyavàn. Savitri was the only child of her father, who was called "Ashvapati." She was exceedingly beautiful and wise. She was growing more and more wise as the moon grows in the first fortnight.. When she was about eighteen years of age, her father sought for a bridegroom, but did not find any one fit to be her husband. Ashvapati was a king, so he searched for a princely bridegroom. He afterwards told his daughter to travel and choose for herself. She went with many attendants and saw many kingdoms on the earth, but did not find any good-natured prince. There was a dethroned king called "Dinmatsen" who had an obedient son named Satyavàn. Dinmatsen and his wife were both blind. This family of three dwelt in a cottage in a forest. Savitri chose Satyavàn for her husband, and immediately returned home to inform her father, who consented to it.

In the mean time Narada descended from Heaven, and went to the King's Palace. Ashvapati was very glad to welcome him. While they were engaged in philosophic conversation Savitri came in and Narada asked where she had been. Ashvapati informed him and Narada then begged her not to marry Satyavàn. She replied that her determination would never alter. Narada and her father tried their best to influence her by telling her that he was dethroned and in reduced circumstances. She refused to heed them. At last Narada explained that Satyavàn would die in a year, and if that would happen, what would she do? Notwithstanding this Savitri stood firm. She said nobody should be defeated at heart, but bear with whatever comes, whether pleasant or painful. "If God has written widowhood on my forehead," she said, "no one is able to wipe it away. God's will shall be done, who will gainsay it? All persons on the Earth except Satyavàn are to me like my father's brothers and sons. Then how could I marry them?"

Narada was pleased with what she said, and ascended to Heaven. Ashvapati made preparations, and started for the forest with his daughter and all her relations. He went to the cottage and explained Savitri's intentions.

Dinmatsen explained that he was poor, blind and dethroned, but finally consented.

So Savitri became the wife of Satyavàn. The King gave them wealth — but they declined it, saying that as they might not enjoy their own riches, they would take nothing from others. The Princess took off her jewels and fine clothes and gave them to her father, and the King returned to his people. Savitri knew the day of her husband's death, which Narada had predicted. She was an obedient wife and when at last only three days were left to him, she could neither sleep nor eat. Sorrow preyed upon her. Her husband and his relations begged her not to fast for she was very delicate. When the last day came, Satyavàn was going as usual to the forest for fuel. Savitri begged him to take her with him. "You are tender and will not be able to walk. You must be very hungry. Eat something and then come if you must." But she urged him, till he sent her to ask the consent of his father and mother. At first they too refused her.

They started for the forest. Her husband said that she had better be at home, for the way was long and difficult. "Should I not be with my dear husband so much as once?" she said. As he was cutting trees with his axe, he was tired, and a venomous snake bit him. He then slept under a great banyan tree, taking his wife's lap under his head instead of a pillow. "Yama," the God of Death, came to her, and asked her to lay her husband aside, that he might take away his soul. "Who are you, and why do you come hither?" said she. He answered her, and she begged him not to separate them, but he would not heed. At last he seized the soul and went away, and she followed him weeping. He looked back and told her to go away and burn the corpse of her husband. "What should I do without my husband," she cried; "wherever my husband's soul is carried I will follow." "You will be tired," he said; "go back and burn the body." "I am your adopted daughter, take me to my mother," she retorted. He desired her to ask anything of him except her husband's soul. She asked that her husband's parents might have their sight. Yama gave it and walked on. He again looked back and told her to return. She said, "How is it that you like to see your daughter a widow?" "Ask for anything," he answered, "except this soul." She desired that Dinmatsen should be restored to his lost kingdom. Yama gave that too, but she did not cease from following. "Go and burn your dead," he cried.

"Oh, this is a spot on your world-wide fame! Death is said to be friendly," she cried.

"Ask me yet a third thing," he entreated.

"I have no brother," she replied. "Oh, bless my father with a son." This also Yama granted, and told her not to follow, but she went on. "Ask me a fourth gift," he said, "and go back to the body." "Venerable father," she said, "I must not be called barren, give me some sons." "They are yours," he said, and went forth, but she followed. He looked back and grew very angry. "Why do you not return?" he said. "How am I to return without the soul of my husband," she said patiently, "you have promised me that I shall not be called barren." Then he remembered that she was not pregnant and repented of his fury. "Go back," he said, "the soul is released." She hurried back to the banyan, in whose shadows she had laid the body before she followed Yama. Again she laid her husband's head upon her lap. In a moment or two he roused and saw the sun shining. She asked her husband why he slept so long, for he knew that his parents would be waiting. He replied that he had been dreaming. Then they hurried home, and found to his great surprise, that his parents had received their sight and that both father and mother were weeping. How glad they were to see their daughter-in-law for the first time with their own eyes! The King who had dethroned them gave everything back, so their last days were full of happiness.

Savitri's father had sons and reigned happily. We therefore observe this day, and worship the banyan as the emblem of eternal marriage.

I shall not be restored to a peaceful mind until I hear that you are recovered from your illness. These two years, since our correspondence commenced, I have never had the misfortune of your letter being put off on account of illness, although I have failed more than once. I sincerely hope and pray to God that my Aunt may soon be able to comfort her niece in her distress.

Your affectionate niece,

ANANDABAI.

The story of Savitri which Anandabai here tells in her own way is one of the most beautiful of the old Hindu epics. Narada or Narad', as the name is pronounced, was a deity who sprang from the hip of Brahma, and who with functions sometimes resembling those of Orpheus, at other times those of Hermes, seems to have interfered constantly in human affairs.

The last letter written from India that I shall offer to my readers is full of character. It shows a girl of seventeen absolutely fearless, because her trust is in God. It gives us some idea of the trials that had already beset her. It hints at the disapprobation of her mother, which was the bitterest drop in her cup, but shows no suspicion of the thousand drawbacks which were to delay her start. In August, 1882, Mrs. Carpenter wrote her a long and careful letter, detailing the manner and expense of coming to America. For the first time the way seemed easy and practicable to Anandabai, and she pours forth her delight as follows.

SERAMPORE, August 12th, 1882.

MY DEAR AUNT, — I proceed to write an answer to your letter dated July 1st, as promised in my last, in which I have acknowledged it. I imparted my joy to you in a few words. As I was reading it, I was in ecstasy, when it fell from my hand. For a while I knew not what to do. I wished I had feathers, to flit at once. On that day I did not eat my food as usual, for my head and heart were full with joy and I thanked the Almighty for the approaching pleasure.

You know at first our intention was that we should both start for America. I remember that you too, a year ago, expressed your wish that we both should go, but now it is altered. After serious deliberation we perceive that it will be very expensive. You can imagine how difficult it is for a small purse to pay for two passengers from India to America. Beside, my husband has an old mother, and younger brothers to care for. I have neither a jealous nature to be hurt by this separation nor any one to care for except my husband. I have had here two dear things above all one of which I have lost (through her disapprobation), and that is my mother. The other is my husband. I have two sisters and one brother. Oh poor mortals! They are under a kinsman's care quite ignorant of this world. So I am untyed. I am not sorry for this, but think myself happy. I am therefore prepared to go alone to America, in company of any respectable family. My husband will be here. Considering the future prospects of my life as a physician I must make up my mind to be separated from my husband.

You have reason to think that very distant voyage will be hazardous for a girl of eighteen because the world is full of frauds and dangers, but dear Aunt, wherever I cast my glance, I see nothing but a straight and smooth way. I fear no miseries. I shrink not at the recollection of dangers, nor do I fear them. Wherever I will be, there will be Heaven for me. I am sure God has created many high souls, like you, who will not neglect me.

Besides, we are never sure that we shall live unseparated for ever. We know not when we shall be condemned to separation. Is it not always possible that one of us will be lost? I give an instance for your satisfaction. One family consisting of four members came to Benares on a pilgrimage two months ago. Unfortunately three of them died of cholera and a helpless girl of eighteen was left behind. What could she do then? She has lost her husband, brother-in-law, mother-in-law. If this life is so transitory like a rose in bloom, why should one depend upon another?

Every one must not ride on another's shoulders but walk on his own feet. Perhaps my husband will follow me, some time after, but I must not wait for him, as time is so precious.

Thousands are too violently attached to the contrary opinions. Hundreds show their own scruples, by urging that I am liable to go astray, and lead an unchaste life when unprotected by any nearest relative. My design meets the approbation of a few, say one or two to a thousand, and they are probably, youths, reformers and patriots. You will easily believe that I, fearing the disapprobation of the many, will desist from my determinate proposal, but it is not so. Though I cannot teach courage, I must not learn cowardice, nor at last leave undone what I so long since determined to do. I am not discouraged. I only wonder at their scruples and their timidity. I am not sorry for their unfavorable opinions. Their opposition strengthens me the more. I promise myself that if my efforts will be successful, I will return to my native country; otherwise I will not see India again. I must not fear but try my best and show all, what we Indian ladies are like. Our antient Indian ladies were very wise, brave, courageous and benevolent, and endurance was their badge. Let it be my badge also. I am sure nothing will harm me, or if it does, it will be for my good. I know that whenever any misfortune has befallen me, it has been profitable for me. As we are all children of one father, none will attempt to deceive or betray me, wheresoever I may be. No one has power to disturb and harm, except He gives it. We have neither the power of devolving misfortunes upon ourselves, nor the power of avoiding them. These must come according to His will. I must launch my fortune like a ship on the ocean of life. To what shore shall it go, to a fertile bank or a barren beach? or will it go to pieces? Let me try to do my duty, whether I be victor or victim. So I have determined, and will start some time in December or January next. Please be so kind as to be there at the time. I am sure you will not seek to deter me from my purpose.

I am impatient to see you and to begin to learn what my country needs. I feel that the movement of my mind is due to the counsels of my husband. What he has taught me, he has so impressed that it will never be effaced.

ANANDABAI.

Mrs. Joshee now began to prepare in earnest for her removal to America. This last letter shows that she had attentively considered all the obstacles in her path, and that while Hindu relatives opposed, her American friends affectionately warned her. In the early part of October she looked forward to travelling with friends of a Mr. and Mrs. Thorburn, probably Missionaries, as she states that Mrs. Thorburn had been a graduate of the Woman's Medical College in Philadelphia and would give her letters to friends there.

On the 17th she writes as if there had been disappointment.

"I am ready, but the company is still to find." "Letters have been sent to all the four quarters." "Missionaries and English people advise me to go directly to New York, to delay in England will be very expensive." "All this waste of time fatigues me."

Nov. 28th, 1882, she continues: —

"Everything is going on through Dr. and Mrs. Thorburn. I do not know how to repay their kindness. I can only thank Him who gives them to me. She has already written to the College in Philadelphia, but I must wait to consult with you.

"I shall go with two English ladies of her acquaintance who will start in February. I am sorry to say that the Mahratta family who were so kind to me in Calcutta are wholly changed since they know I am going. My husband wrote them, when we could no longer keep it secret. They have only one child, a boy of eight, so they had adopted me as a daughter. They did a great deal for me. I still think them kind and good. Their opposition is due to tender hearts, fearful minds, and foolish superstition. They are doing all they can to prevent my going to America, but I cannot blame them. I have been like a child to them, dutiful, and I wish to continue so.

"God has given me two precious things, my husband and my aunt. You will see how I have hardened my heart, when I tell you that I will be happy with you, though I am separated from him. I have given all my cares and anxieties to Him who is the only Soul. He who separates us will bring us together again."

Jan'y 16th, 1883, she writes:—

"You must be expecting to hear that I have found my escort and know when I shall start, but nothing is settled. I have been to Mrs. Thorburn on the first and twelfth of this month. The last time I was advised to join a medical class which is shortly to be opened in Calcutta under the supervision of Dr. Thorburn. This was unexpected, and I could not reconcile myself to it. I told them I could not change my plans. Mrs. Thorburn said she would do her best for me, but knew of no escort. I found her wholly changed, and wrote to my husband.

"'I saw Mrs. Thorburn at the appointed hour. She has disappointed me. Never mind, the opposition of friends brings God to my side. I am not discouraged.' Before he received this, he had called on Dr. Thorburn, and shared my disappointment. Instead of losing courage he went off to plan some other way, so I am glad to tell you, that I will start early in February. My husband will go as far as Madras or Aden, till he can leave me with a trusty friend. Dear Aunt, every day I learn something new. What I thought to be true yesterday I find to be false to-day, and something else to-morrow. God's ways are not known to man. Do not think I have anything to say against Dr. and Mrs. Thorburn. They have been very kind and took a lively interest in my plans. They may have received bitter letters from my relatives, or they may not find me fit for encouragement. Be that as it may, I will see America, the dream of my life, and I will stand or fall as I deserve.

"On the 12th was a holiday, on which I had gone uninvited to Calcutta to distribute sesamum-seed and earthen pots. The Mahrattas treated me so unkindly that I could not stay. He showed such a temper that I bitterly repented going. I do not blame them, for they had treated me like their own daughter. They think it is my rashness or thoughtlessness, which prompts a thing so hap-hazardous! I have so many difficulties and disappointments that I have not answered your last two letters."

Jan. 23d, 1883, she writes, "I am glad to say, that I shall start on the steamer 'Quetta,' leaving Calcutta viâ England on February 17th."

On the 30th she says again, "Nothing is changed." On the 13th of February she writes from Serampore: —

"I am afraid you will not think me truthful. Last time I spoke of one thing, this time of another, and who knows? it may be something else next time! It would be madness to expect you to believe me, when I cannot believe myself. Since I wrote Dr. Thorburn sent a letter saying, "At last, we have made a very good arrangement to send Mrs. Joshee with a party of ladies by the 'City of Calcutta,'" etc. My husband thanked him, but did not accept the offer. He soon called on Dr. Thorburn and told him of my plans. The Doctor said the Steamers of the Line my husband intended me to take were not good. Many rough people travelled on them and he thought I was too young to go that way. He added that the 'City of Calcutta' would carry a student of the Philadelphia College much interested in my plans. My husband thought that it would be too expensive to send me first class, but the Doctor assured him that if I went with a party of Missionaries, the difference would be very small. So my husband came home, and the next day sent the Doctor a letter; in which he said, "If this lady takes my wife as a companion to please herself we shall be very much obliged, but if it is only to please you, and there is any grudge, we would rather depend upon Him who has created us all.'

"So we have postponed starting for America. I was confounded, but what would people say of me if I despised this offered help? How will it end? Sometimes our measures bring about the very evils they are intended to prevent. I am ashamed to speak of starting. If God pleases, I will start by the 'City of

Calcutta' about the first of April. I am not sure of anything. I am not a performer of anything. I am only His instrument. The whole day and night I dream only of seeing you."

Such extracts as these might be multiplied many times. It seemed as if Anandabai's difficulties would never come to an end, but with what sweetness and serenity she encountered them! A rare union of qualities, for many who do not fail in sweetness can hardly be called serene. How touching is the humility with which she defends the Thorburns and the Mahratta family to whom she was so closely bound! *They* are not to blame, they have received bitter letters from her family, they do not find *her* fit for encouragement! all she undertakes must seem to *them* "hap-hazardous!" However it seemed, it came truly of the "counsels of God."

And now she had come to the crisis of her life. Let us consider what manner of woman she really was and what experience she had had.

Of all the adventurous tribes who travelled southwards she came of those who from their hardihood, endurance and enterprise had constituted the first military order in the country. In this military order of Rajpoots a still more intelligent and adventurous gens originated, and from this her ancestors were born. The record she believed her family to have kept for two thousand years was the record of exceptionally brave, stalwart and loyal men. The mantle of one of these men, distinguished by royal gifts and the founder of her family, had fallen upon her, young and tender as she seemed. Her experience of life had been varied. Her childhood had been passed between Kalyan and Poonah. At Kalyan, she was the daughter of a large landholder everywhere respected and beloved, who was himself highly intelligent and quite as distinct a monotheist as if he had publicly enrolled himself among the "Lions."

At Poonah she lived in a princely house in a city of refinement and resources. In neither place could she ever have encountered a bold glance or a disrespectful word.

Out of this serene atmosphere her marriage snatched her. Bombay was too large a city to treat her as she deserved, when her mountain habits attracted attention.

The Island of Cutch had introduced her to everything that was repellent. When she fixed her affections upon a family of her own people in Calcutta she found them wholly wanting in the sincere and simple piety which had characterized her father.

At Serampore, where her husband was postmaster, her position was prominent enough to draw the attention of the whole native population. No one was inclined to aid her. It was at Serampore that Henry Martyn lived, and the Baptist College seemed still to glow with the fire of his saintly life. The Christians, European and native, did not wish her to go abroad unless she would submit to baptism before she went. The Brahmins reviled her for even entertaining the intention, and rejoiced over every fresh obstacle. As the rumors of repeated disappointment and repeated fresh endeavors rose or fell the excitement increased. The Joshees lived in the Post-Office building. At last, the disturbance seriously interfered with the public business. At all hours the building was thronged and surrounded by groups of Bengalis of all castes, whose noisy declamation and angry gestures seemed likely to reflect discredit upon the office itself. In this condition of things, Gopal proposed to get permission to make a public statement of their intentions in the College Hall. He was very much surprised to find that Anandabai preferred to make the statement herself, but he yielded.

The "courage of her convictions," which carried her to the platform on the 24th of February, 1883, has not yet been properly estimated in this country. It is not likely that any woman, either native or European, had ever addressed a public audience in that place. For a Brahmin woman to appear in public at all was, as we have seen from Anandabai's Calcutta experience, a grave misdemeanor. For her to appear in order to justify her own departure from the ways of her fathers was doubtless a graver still, and if it had not been for the general excitement, it is doubtful whether the use of the hall would have been granted.

Be that as it might, when the hour came the hall was crowded. A large number of natives had assembled, and with them a few Europeans. Among the latter was a certain Col. Hans Mattison, American Consul General in India, who was stationed at Calcutta and had from the very first felt a deep interest in her. The Rev. Mr. Summers, of the Baptist College, presided at the meeting. Anandabai made no preparation and had no notes. If it had not been for the affectionate care of Col. Mattison, we should have lost this remarkable address. Some months after her arrival in this country Anandabai received half a dozen printed copies of it from Bombay, without having the slightest idea from whom it came.

Omitting her Sanscrit quotations from Manu, and dropping a few paragraphs consisting of repetitions, I copy here the little pamphlet issued by the "Native Opinion Press," of Bombay. Certainly if it was ever read in the palace at Poonah it must have touched her mother's heart.

LADIES AND GENTLEMEN, — I stand here to fail, as I am not likely to succeed. I am however exceedingly thankful to you for the trouble you have taken to attend this meeting. You may have gathered here anxiously to hear of some interesting subject, but I am afraid you will be disappointed to hear me talking of an uninteresting one. But what should I do? There is no remedy. Had it been in my power to give you a pleasing address, I would have done so. The only attempt I have ever made to speak in public is this. I have studied but a little while and the language which I intend to speak in, is not only foreign but thoroughly out of command, and entirely unused. I am therefore liable to make thousands of blunders even in grammar. Many of those who are present here, are mere school-boys who will rejoice to find that I am not equal to themselves: the young will laugh and the old will pity my ignorance.

I wish I had better knowledge of the language to

attract the attention of you all. Pardon me for the disappointment you will have to suffer. I do not wish to tire you by a long preface, and as I want your unfatigued attention to a long narration, I beg to discontinue it.

I wish to thank the College authorities for allowing me to stand here, more especially the Rev. Mr. Summers for presiding.

Our subject to-day is, "My future visit to America, and public inquiries regarding it."

I am asked hundreds of questions about my going to America. I take this opportunity to answer some of them.

1. Why do I go to America?
2. Are there no means to study in India?
3. Why do I go alone?
4. Shall I not be excommunicated on my return?
5. What shall I do if misfortune befall me?
6. Why should I do what is not done by any of my sex?

1. I go to America because I wish to study medicine. I now address the ladies present here, who will be the better judges of the importance of female medical assistance in India. I never consider this subject without being surprised that none of those societies so laudably established in India for the promotion of sciences and female education have ever

thought of sending one of their female members into the most civilized parts of the world to procure thorough medical knowledge, in order to open here a College for the instruction of women in medicine. There is probably no country so barbarous as India that would not disclose all her wants and try to stand on her own feet. The want of female physicians in India is keenly felt in every quarter. Ladies both European and Native are naturally averse to expose themselves in cases of emergency to treatment by doctors of the other sex. There are some female doctors in India from Europe and America, who being foreigners and different in manners, customs and language, have not been of such use to our women as they might. As it is very natural that Hindu ladies who love their own country and people should not feel at home with the natives of other countries, we Indian women absolutely derive no benefit from these foreign ladies.

They indeed have the appearance of supplying our need, but the appearance is delusive. In my humble opinion there is a growing need for Hindu lady doctors in India, and I volunteer to qualify myself for one.

2. Are there no means to study in India?

No. I do not mean to say there are *no* means, but the difficulties are many and great. There is one College at Madras, and midwifery classes are opened in all the Presidencies; but the education imparted is defective and not sufficient, as the instructors who teach the classes are conservative, and to some extent jealous. I do not find fault with them. That is the characteristic of the male sex. We must put up with this inconvenience until we have a class of educated ladies to relieve these men.

I am neither a Christian nor a Brahmo. To continue to live as a Hindu and go to school in any part of India is very difficult. A convert who wears an English dress is not so much stared at. Native Christian ladies are free from the opposition or public scandal which Hindu ladies like myself have to meet within and without the *zenana*. If I go alone by train or in the street some people come near to stare and ask impertinent questions to annoy me. Example is better than precept. Some few years ago, when I was in Bombay, I used to go to school. When people saw me going with my books in my hands, they had the goodness to put their heads out of the window just to have a look at me. Some stopped their carriages for the purpose. Others walking in the streets stood laughing, and crying out so that I could hear:—

"What is this? Who is this lady who is going to school with boots and stockings on?"

"Does not this show that the Kali Uga has stamped its character on the minds of the people?"

Ladies and gentlemen, you can easily imagine what

effect questions like these would have on your minds if you had been in my place!

Once it happened that I was obliged to stay in school for some time, and go twice a day for my meals to the house of a relation.

Passers-by, whenever they saw me going, gathered round me. Some of them made fun, and were convulsed with laughter. Others, sitting respectably in their verandahs, made ridiculous remarks, and did not feel ashamed to throw pebbles at me. The shop-keepers and venders spit at the sight of me, and made gestures too indecent to describe. I leave it to you to imagine what was my condition at such a time, and how I could gladly have burst through the crowd to make my home nearer!

Yet the boldness of my Bengali brethren cannot be exceeded, and is still more serious to contemplate than the instances I have given from Bombay. Surely it deserves pity! If I go to take a walk on the strand, Englishmen are not so bold as to look at me. Even the soldiers are never troublesome; but the Babus lay bare their levity by making fun of everything. "Who are you?" "What caste do you belong to?" "Whence do you come?" "Where do you go?" are, in my opinion, questions that should not be asked by strangers. There are some educated native Christians here in Serampore who are suspicious; they are still wondering whether I am married or a widow; a woman of bad character or excommunicated! Dear audience, does it become my native and Christian brethren to be so uncharitable? Certainly not. I place these unpleasant things before you, that those whom they concern most may rectify them, and those who have never thought of the difficulties may see that I am not going to America through any whim or caprice.

3. Why do I go alone? It was at first the intention of my husband and myself to go together, but we were forced to abandon this thought. We have not sufficient funds; but that is not the only reason. There are others still more important and convincing. My husband has his aged parent and younger brothers and sisters to support. You will see that his departure would throw those dependent upon him into the arena of life, penniless and alone. How cruel and inhuman it would be for him to take care of one soul and reduce so many to starvation! Therefore I go alone.

4. Shall I not be excommunicated when I return to India? Do you think I should be filled with consternation at this threat? I do not fear it in the least. Why should I be cast out, when I have determined to live there exactly as I do here? I propose to myself to make no change in my customs and manners, food or dress. I will go as a Hindu, and come back here to live as a Hindu. I will not

increase my wants, but be as plain and simple as my forefathers, and as I am now. If my countrymen wish to excommunicate me, why do they not do it now? They are at liberty to do so. I have come to Bengal and to a place where there is not a single Maharastra. Nobody here knows whether I behave according to my customs and manners, or not. Let us therefore cease to consider what may never happen, and what, when it may happen, will defy human speculation.

5. What will I do if misfortune befall me? Some persons fall into the error of exaggerated declamation, by producing in their talk examples of national calamities and scenes of extensive misery which are found in books rather than in the world, and which, as they are horrid, are ordained to be rare. A man or a woman who *wishes to act* does not look at that dark side which others easily foresee. On necessary and inevitable evils which crush him or her to dust, all dispute is vain. When they happen they must be endured, but it is evident they are oftener dreaded than experienced. Whether perpetual happiness can be obtained in any way, this world will never give us an opportunity to decide. But this we may say, we do not always find visible happiness in proportion to visible means. It is not a thing which may be divided among a certain number of men. It depends upon feeling. If Death be only miserable, why should

some rejoice at it, while others lament? On the other hand, Death and Misery come alike to good and bad, virtuous and vicious, rich and poor, travellers and housekeepers; all are confounded in the misery of famine, and not greatly distinguished in the fury of faction. No man is able to prevent any catastrophe. Misery and Death are always near, and should be expected. When the result of any hazardous work is good, we praise the enterprise which undertook it; when it is evil, we blame the imprudence. The world is always ready to call enterprise imprudence when fortune changes.

Some say that those who stay at home are happy, but where does their happiness lie? Happiness is not a ready-made thing to be enjoyed because one desires it. Some minds are so fond of variety that pleasure if permanent would be insupportable, and they solicit happiness by courting distress. To go to foreign countries is not bad, but in some respects better than to stay in one place. The study of people and places is not to be neglected. Ignorance when voluntary is criminal. In going to foreign countries, we may enlarge our comprehension, perfect our knowledge, or recover lost arts. Every one must do what he thinks right. Every man has owed much to others. His effort ought to be to repay what he has received. Let us follow the advice of Goldsmith who says: "Learn to pursue virtue of a man who is blind, who never takes a step without first examining the ground with his staff." I take my Almighty Father for my staff, who will examine the path before He leads me further. I can find no better staff than He.

And last you ask me, why I should do what is not done by any of my sex? To this I can only say, that society has a right to our work as individuals.

It is very difficult to decide the duties of individuals. It is enough that the good of one must be the good of all. If anything seems best for all mankind, each one of us must try to bring it about. According to Manu, the desertion of duty is an unpardonable sin. So I am surprised to hear that I should not do this, because it has not been done by others. Our ancestors whose names have become immortal had no such notions in their heads. I ask my Christian friends, "Do you think you would have been saved from your sins, if Jesus Christ, according to your notions, had not sacrificed his life for you all?" Did *he* shrink at the extreme penalty that he bore while doing good? No, I am sure you will never admit that *he* shrank! Neither did our ancient kings "*Shibi*" and "*Mayuradhwaj.*" To desist from duty because we fear failure or suffering is not just. *We must try.* Never mind whether we are victors or victims. Manu has divided people into three classes. The meanest are those who never attempt anything for fear of failure. Those who begin, and are disheartened by the first obstacles, come next; but those who begin, and persevere through failure and obstacle, are those who win.

The greater the difficulty, the greater our courage. Never let us desist from what we once begin.

I have done. I am afraid I have exhausted your patience for which I beg to be excused.

Thus she pleaded. Let us imagine a young American girl in her situation! Is there anything in the spirit of the discourse that we should wish to change? The expression could not have been the same, for expression is born of experience, of our own experience, and that of generations that have gone before; but in all that is "pure womanly," all that shows loyalty to conviction and courage to endure, no American mother need ask more from her child than Anandabai Joshee was able to give.

She writes again from Serampore, Feb. 27th, 1883:—

"I gave a lecture on the 24th instant at the Serampore College, concerning my journey, and the public inquiries regarding it. There was a large gathering of natives, and a few Europeans."

On March 6th she adds:—

"After hearing of my lecture Mr. H. E. M. James, the Director General of the Post Offices of India, wrote to my husband: 'I was very glad to hear that Mrs. Joshee has made her débût, and has succeeded. Pray give her my congratulations. I wish her every success. In recognition of her courage and public spirit, permit me to offer the enclosed check for one hundred Rupees, which may be useful to her.'"

The money sent by Mr. James was more necessary than many of Anandabai's friends would suspect. She never asked for aid, and it is only since her death that we have learned with sorrow that the massive bracelets and bangles given to her by her father when she married were quietly sold to provide her passage money to America.

"I was sorry," wrote Mrs. Summers, "not to have been present at your lecture on Saturday afternoon. I had to conduct a Woman's Bible Class just at that time, but my husband told me that it was a great success, so accept my congratulations."

"I have received a good many letters from other friends," she writes. "Mrs. Thorburn has written me a letter of congratulation. One month is still to pass." The sailing of the steamship was, however, deferred from the 30th of March to the 7th of April. The poor child's courage was almost spent. On the 3d she continues:—

"Overjoyed with the approach of the happy time to which I have looked forward so long, I sit down to write what may be my last letter. Everything is settled. I feel better since I know that there is nothing to do but embark. I have come to Calcutta with my husband. We are with a Mahratta friend, who is young and kind. I have just come from the Consul-General of the United States, who has given me two letters of introduction. I shall go on board on the evening of the 6th, and we shall start the next morning. The time draws near in which we shall be in one country and one place. Every moment shortens the time."

On the 8th of April, 1883, Gopal wrote to Mr. Carpenter: —

"My wife sailed yesterday morning, by the 'City of Calcutta,' in the company of many ladies who were strangers to her. She was to have sailed on Monday, the 9th; but early in the morning of Friday I received word that she must be ready to start on Saturday. We had invitations for the next three days, but could only decline them and hasten to get ready. She was not introduced to the ladies with whom she was to travel until she reached the ship, and even then her reception was cold indeed. Although at the eleventh hour, I advised my wife to expect nothing from them, but to trust to Him who has made us both.

My dear sir, I took good care of her until her departure, and now I hand over this precious charge to you and your worthy wife."

In the letters that I have quoted, three distinct things are evident. First, Anandabai's own originality and nobleness of mind and conduct; second, a sort of Fatalism, common to Oriental people; and third, the use of certain phrases, or proverbs, evidently taken from the more cynical lips of her husband. This last trait will not be so evident to my readers as to myself, for I dropped the phrases out of my text wherever the repetition threatened to be tiresome.

Of Anandabai's journey to America we know very little. She sailed on the 7th of April, 1883, and arrived in New York on the 4th of June. On account of the engagements of the party with which she travelled she remained a week in London, and eight days at Queenstown on account of some matter connected with the steamer. The circumstances of her journey must have been evident to those who had charge of her; and to us who know her it seems incredible that she could have passed some sixty days in the society of any number of people without awakening in some one a profound interest. In speaking of her journey she said, briefly, that she was always under restraint, as those she travelled with could never be convinced that she would remain a Hindu in her faith, and felt it their duty to press the claims of the Christian religion. She did not feel at home in London, where she was asked to add the attractions of her finest saree and best jewels to those of any social gathering in which the missionaries naturally desired to rouse deeper interest. At New York she was met by her nearest friends, Mr. and Mrs. Carpenter, of Roselle, New Jersey. She had already adopted them into her heart, and never from the first seems to have had a doubt or reserve in regard to them. She remained at Roselle from June 4th to Oct. 1st, 1883, and in these four months stole into the hearts of those who met her. Before leaving India she had expressed a fear that she might become tedious, or seem vulgar, from her ignorance of our manners. Instead of that, she was everywhere a "well-spring of delight!" On her first arrival her perfect dignity was never sacrificed to the indulgence in curious questions, or rude stares, which were so freely bestowed upon herself, yet she seemed to miss nothing.

After a little she pursued her Sanscrit studies, regardless of the presence of visitors. She was often called off to sing her lovely little Hindu songs, or to recite verses in some of the strange tongues she knew. She was always gracefully courteous, but the words of approbation or admiration with which her efforts were greeted never seemed to touch her. Quick to note every fact presented to her, grateful for every bit of information, — flattering words never seemed to be understood. "I do not care for words," she sometimes said; "I know how my friends feel without them." Mrs. Carpenter was at first surprised that Anandabai never addressed her by name; but she soon found that, from the Hindu point of view, such an address would have been disrespectful. A visit to Tiffany's gave Anandabai great pleasure; and she showed such knowledge and appreciation of everything Oriental, that the finest goods were exhibited as if to a favored customer, and she was urged to prolong and repeat her visit.

Anandabai always said that this summer was the happiest of her life. I think she spoke the simple truth; but she would have been very much surprised if any one had pointed out the true sources of that happiness. Yet she was far too truthful not to have recognized them, had the attempt been made. She was with those who really loved her, and who asked no greater privilege than to aid her in her plans. No more restraints foreign to her experience, like the customs of Bengal; no more bitter letters from envious or dissatisfied kinsfolk, — nay, still farther, none of the thousand observances and deferences required of the married woman by the customs of her country. Every morning she religiously applied the scarlet paste in a little round patch to her forehead, which proclaimed that she was a wife. Every day she added some loving or witty words to the letter sent by every mail to her husband in Serampore, but there all ended; for the rest she was as free as a child, and like a child she glided about the house humming her Hindu songs. She was never weary of talking about her dear native land, and this summer she gave a great treat to her Roselle friends by improvising for their benefit a Hindu feast. Mrs. Carpenter was at this time living in a large house. All the furniture was removed from the dining-room, and the smooth inlaid floor was ornamented and divided by delicate stripes of red and white about four inches wide. Including Anandabai, there were eighteen guests, and eighteen squares were drawn in red and white, one for each guest, surrounding a central square. The powders had been brought from India. The red was first applied in a broad band, and then the white was sifted over it from a brass cylinder, perforated with small holes in a pretty pattern. The effect was like that produced on ladies' dresses by a band of white lace applied over crimson silk. Within the four corners of the central square were drawn intricate geometrical figures in the two colors, and scroll-like lines on the outer corners of the individual squares formed a pretty recess for the fresh green leaves of the buttonwood. These had been sewed together to do service as plates, instead of the long banana leaf which would have been used in India. Travellers in India have not unfrequently seen á similar delicate tracery in colored sand on the open road as they have approached sacred buildings, but it has seldom fallen to their lot to participate in a native feast. Smooth pieces of board were placed near the walls within each square to take the place of chairs. Small plates were set near the leaves in the corner to hold rice and curry. Sweetmeats were also served in small dishes. The guests half reclined upon the boards.

The ladies were all dressed by Anandabai in bright-bordered Indian sarees, which she took from her own wardrobe. The food, consisting only of fruit and vegetables, had been first prepared and then served by her own delicate hands. A

Sanscrit prayer was reverently offered, and then eighteen dishes of the peculiar Hindu cookery were followed by coffee. As soon as each guest was supplied and the surplus carried away from the dining-room, Anandabai entered the square reserved for her, and prepared to teach her guests how to eat like a Hindu.

None of them had dared to begin till she took her seat, for neither knife, fork, nor spoon was on the board. Anandabai would pick up a morsel, bring it a few inches from her plate, and then with a dexterous twist of her fingers toss it into her mouth. It seemed to fly magically to the right spot. "To miss," she said, "would be vulgar." After dinner, the guests repaired to the parlor, where a large mat had been spread, and huge white cushions had been provided for the ladies to lean upon. Against these the rich colors of the Indian sarees made a pretty show. Every married lady had the scarlet mark on her forehead, and such bangles, necklaces, and other ornaments as Anandabai had been able to procure. To the ladies, half reclining on the mat, and to the gentlemen standing or squatting Hindu fashion on the floor, Anandabai distributed bouquets of flowers, and on the back of each right hand she left with her dainty finger a trace of attar of roses, which she took from a phial of green and gold.

The company were then sprinkled with rose-water from a silver vessel, and Anandabai sat down, evidently considering that her work was done. Not so her guests; they had heard that Oriental dinners were wont to conclude with song, and at their earnest entreaty one tender ditty or one birdlike caprice followed another, until all were tired. It was a little singular that on this occasion all the guests seemed to approve of the unwonted cookery.

Not once did Anandabai show any signs of home-sickness. Little did she know what she promised when she told her people that in America she "would eat and drink, live or die as a Hindu." Did she begin to see how hard it would be? When the letters from India came, her dear little face would light up like a child's, and for days after she would go humming her sweet tunes about the house, until loneliness began to make itself felt, and then she was silent till the next mail day. Anandabai could talk to the old, amuse the middle-aged, and play gently with the children, as no one else could. The children thought they were going to teach her to play jack-stones. The skill of her very beautiful hands was always something wonderful to Western eyes. In botanical analysis, or delicate surgery, they served her well. With the jack-stones she had been at home from childhood, and turning her palm inside out she would catch the whole six or eight in the hollow. Very few persons thought Anandabai beautiful at first sight. Almost every one found her complexion darker than had been expected, and her form less graceful; but to every one, sometime during the years that followed, there came a sudden revelation, a day when the soul seemed to flash through the flesh, to burn in the dark eyes, to inform the very finger-tips, and sway every fold of the wonderful dress.

That summer she had the offer of a scholarship in the Homœopathic College in New York, but on the whole she and her friends thought it best that she should begin with a four years' course in the Woman's Medical College of Pennsylvania, and it was gratefully declined. At this College Anandabai was matriculated Oct. 3d, 1883. She had reached Philadelphia on Friday, September 28th. On Saturday, Dr. Bodley held a reception for her. The good Dean's heart had been won at first sight. There was naturally a great deal of curiosity concerning Anandabai as soon as she appeared in the streets of Philadelphia. There had been Turkish and Syrian and Chinese pupils at the College, but Anandabai was the first pupil who had come from a foreign land wearing its native dress and preserving her native habits. It is greatly to the credit of our people, that she was never once seriously annoyed by their curiosity. In her own country she had worn a "divided" saree. The shawl passing between the legs produced the effect of Turkish trousers. As this would not have been suitable to our climate, she consulted her Pundits, and an ancient form of the Mahratta dress was found, that could be worn over warm underclothing.

As soon as she left Calcutta, Anandabai assumed a "union suit" of flannel, over that a union suit of cotton, then a skirt of flannel, one or two white skirts, and a dress made with a plain round waist, coat sleeves, and full skirt.

This latter article was for protection; the waist of it took the place of the queer little jacket which covered the chest, and sustained her breasts, in her native country. Her saree, which draped her entire figure, concealed the skirt.

The saree is best described as a long shawl; its material varies according to work and weather, and ranges in value from the finest camel's hair, or Dacca muslin wrought with solid gold thread, to thin bordered cottons that scarcely cost a rupee. This shawl is never less than forty inches wide and four yards long, and according to its thickness, varies from four to eight yards in length. One end of Anandabai's saree was brought round the full skirt I have described, and tied by both corners at the waist line on the right side, in a small hard knot. The other was then passed under the left arm, to the back and over the right shoulder, across the bosom obliquely. The upper border was then snugly tucked in at the left side under the border which had been first tied round the waist. This allowed a good part of the length of the long shawl to fall diagonally over the right arm, and down before her person, displaying the broad bands of the border. The yards of material yet to be disposed of were gathered by the dexterous use of her hand into regular plaits, and tucked into the girdle under the falling drapery in front. This caused the handsome broad fringed end of the saree to hang in graceful folds just above the instep.

When finally arranged, no part of the under dress was visible, except that which covered the left arm and shoulder and a portion of the left side of the bust. The right arm, which sustained most of the drapery, came slightly into view, and in ordinary weather the shawl, where it crossed the right shoulder, was lifted so as to cover the head, and was the only protection worn in the street. Anandabai's sarees were made of cotton, cotton and silk, cotton and gold, silk, silk and gold, and camel's hair decorated with silk and with silk and gold, and, in her most superb dress, with gold only. In this country, of course, she relinquished the padded and divided sandal of her native hills, and wore warm woollen or cotton stockings with buttoned boots. This dress was not complete till ear-rings, a nose-ring, and several necklaces, many bangles, anklets, and finger-rings were added. The longer Anandabai lived in America the less she liked to wear her ornaments, or rather those ornaments which, like the ear-rings and the nose-ring, recalled a savage condition of society. When *she* wore them they did not offend me. The spray of pearl flowers, with hearts of rubies and emeralds, which lay across her upper lip was *called* a "nose-ring," but it was not a "ring" at all. It was made of whole pearls lightly strung upon wire, and was hooked into the left nostril so near the cheek that the insertion was not visible, and the ornament seemed to harmonize with her modest, childlike bearing. It was rather like a spray of blossoms playfully caught and held between her lips. Her most valuable anklets and bangles, the gift of her father at the time of her marriage, had been sold in India, as we know, to furnish the money for her voyage to America, but she preserved some heirlooms, which were very curious, and greatly resembled old Aztec work. The description I have given of her draperies applies to her ordinary wear, and will be readily understood by reference to her photographs; but the arrangement varied somewhat according to the weather and the weight and length of the material employed. I questioned her carefully once as to the healthfulness of the native dress. She thought the saree very inconvenient for a working woman: it must be thrown back when the wearer was busy, and then the person was not protected; but she never experienced the slightest inconvenience from wearing it as a student until her lungs began to fail. Then she found it very hard to carry the drapery upon her right arm, and acknowledged that the left side needed more covering.

About the time that Anandabai arrived in this country an article was published in Frank Leslie's Illustrated Newspaper drawing public attention to her. It was written by her friend Hans Mattison, the American Consul General at Calcutta.

"We give on this page," he says, "a portrait of Mrs. Anandabai Joshee, a Brahmin of high social standing, who has recently produced a sensation in India by breaking away from Hindu thought and custom and announcing her determination to secure for herself all the advantages which are enjoyed by women in Christian lands. When it is remembered that the Brahmins are forbidden to cross the ocean, to eat food which has not been prepared by Brahmins, or to drink water touched by European hands, and that the violation of these orders involves severe penalties, Mrs. Joshee's heroism becomes strikingly apparent.

"In her parting address she said: 'We do not endeavor to modify the action of the elements, or to fix the destiny of kingdoms. It is our business to consider what human beings can do, each striving to secure his own happiness by assuring the happiness of others within his own circle, however narrow that may be.'"

Dr. Bodley had done well to summon the best women of Philadelphia to meet her new pupil at the outset. In this way a solid foundation of personal interest was secured. Her friend, Mrs. Carpenter, came with Anandabai, and remained a day or two to settle her in her own home. At first the little room, with its warm stove, and cooking utensils brought from India, seemed to promise a certain cosey comfort for the winter, and to sustain Anandabai's resolution to live in all things like a

Hindu. But the stove smoked, — it was one thing to kindle the responsive charcoal on the little pottery brazier in Hindustan, and another to deal with the tiresome anthracite in America: the fire went out. If the brass vessels had to be cleaned and the various kinds of "dal" cooked, there could not be time for necessary study.

Dr. Bodley saw how it was; and long before her one line of complaint, "I feel very lonesome," had time to settle into serious homesickness, she was removed to the Dean's house, where she was granted all the privileges of a dear daughter. "How kind the Americans are!" she wrote; and as Christmas approached, and she prepared to spend it at Roselle, she added, "perhaps *you* would not know, dear Aunt, how delightful it is to get ready to go home!"

A female physician who had been very kind to Anandabai died about this time at Elizabeth in New Jersey.

"Is she taken away from those who love her dearly and need her so badly?" our little Hindu wrote. "What a mystery this world is! Happy to-day, miserable to-morrow! How true that our deepest sorrows flow from our deepest affections. What an instrument of torture one's own heart is!"

She often spoke of "seeing" this friend as simply, and with as little thought of possible contradiction, as if the Doctor had walked in from the street in the flesh to call upon her.

She returned to the College, Jan. 2nd, 1884, in deep distress of mind, occasioned by a letter received from a most bitter enemy in India. She could not listen to her lectures, and writes as follows a day or two after: —

"My face was clouded by my indignation. My friends said my color changed from red to blue, and thought I was sick. All at once a beautiful young lady with a sweet voice came and sat down by me, and pressing my hand with her own, said, —

"'Dear child, do not despond. Providence is just and merciful, and means you no harm. Have courage to endure many more such things. Do you not remember how I was persecuted in the presence of my husband the king? Be true and faithful.' Then she seemed to disappear. I felt her presence though I could no longer see her, and was comforted."

In February, 1884, Mrs. Joshee was so ill of diphtheria, that for a short time her life was despaired of. The best medical attendance, a trained nurse, and the loving care of Dean Bodley and Dr. Schultze saved her. It was during this spring that Anandabai gave an address before a Ladies' Missionary Society upon the subject of "Early Marriages." I think it tried the patience of those who were interested in her very severely. I have never seen any abstract of her remarks, but if she favored early marriages was it strange? She had been married at nine years. All the happiness of her life had flowed from the instruction of her husband, and from that liberal sympathy which she supposed to move him in assisting her to come to this country. When she arrived, she found our papers full of conjugal quarrels, and applications for divorce. Not in one year nor twenty could she be expected to solve the problems whose very existence filled her with disgust. At this time she was taken frequently to schools, asylums, and public institutions, and wherever she could learn anything, she was delighted to go. A visit to Barnum's Circus gave her no pleasure whatever.

At this time she had a narrow escape from death at the Morristown Insane Asylum, where she had gone to witness a post-mortem dissection. She lingered in the operating-room for some reason, when an insane woman who had escaped unobserved from her attendants to watch the operation, seized one of the sharpest instruments, and approaching Mrs. Joshee announced her intention of operating upon her. The woman stood between Anandabai and the door, and only those who knew the latter well, can guess at the cool smile and wise speech which disarmed and held the maniac, until an attendant appeared. I remember hearing with some interest, soon after she began her studies, that she was the only one of her class who remained through a lecture accompanied by a post-mortem dissection of an infant. When I spoke to her about it, she only said, —

"It would have been better if it had not been a baby."

During the summer vacation of 1884, Anandabai went with some relatives of Mrs. Carpenter to Saratoga. Every step of the journey was full of meaning to the silent little traveller. Her rippling laugh frequently told of her pleasure on the way. Arrived, it pleased her very much to see the ladies going about without bonnets; the younger going to the springs morning and evening without even a veil over the beautiful hair. Here, too, she made her first acquaintance with North American Indians. In one young squaw she took a great interest, talking with her about manners and customs, and receiving from her several friendly gifts.

"Ever since I left Roselle," she now writes to Mrs. Carpenter, "I have not spent a day without my new companion the headache. Every movement gives me pain; but you need not worry about it, for I do not let it interfere with anybody's happiness, nor even with my own. I enjoy the blissful quietude of all country places. One day at Troy we had some cucumber pickles; the pickles looked unnaturally green. I suspected copper in them. No one could tell me about them, so I took a needle and ran it into one of the cucumbers. In a few minutes I was satisfied, for the needle had turned bright red."

In October she resumed her college work, and writes as follows:—

PHILADELPHIA, PA., Oct. 9th, 1884.

MY DEAR AUNT,—Excuse me for not writing earlier. The College opened on Thursday, October 2d; the opening address was by Professor Parish; it was a charming lecture, useful and interesting to every individual, the subject being Practical Hygiene. It was timely, and benefitted me as well as the general public. He had a large audience. The day after, my work began; I have to attend all the lectures except those on Materia Medica and Surgery, which I take up next year. I work from fifteen to sixteen hours daily. The day after College began, Mrs. Smith and I went to the Electrical Exhibition in the evening, and enjoyed it very much. I enjoy my studies more than ever. Professor White came only three days ago, so we had our first lecture on Physic yesterday. I am grieved to tell you I am to lose an excellent friend and teacher. The sickness of Dr. Emily Du Bois, Demonstrator of Anatomy, was sudden to us all; but *she knew it before.* Faithful, prompt, and thorough, she neglected her own self.

I have not taken the money on the checque just received from the James fund. As I had enough trouble in trying to have another cashed, on account of the wrong spelling of my name, I did not try to borrow any more trouble that day. I have so little time to spare. I have not a cent with me, but owe a little to Mrs. Smith, and cannot get to clinics for the same reason. I have had a very severe cold for a week, and am aching all over.

This remark about the James fund is the only allusion to be found in her correspondence to a matter which must have afforded her sincere pleasure.

It will be remembered that Mr. James, the Director General of the Post Offices in India, had sent one hundred rupees to Anandabai, after her address at Serampore, and expressed his pleasure at her success; he did not lose sight of her, and some time after her arrival in this country

Mr. Joshee sent his wife the following circular, which had been published in the Calcutta papers, and was written by Mr. James:—

"A young Brahmin lady has recently gone to America to study medicine, and qualify herself as a medical attendant for native ladies.

"In doing this, she and her husband have made great pecuniary sacrifices, and her income barely suffices for necessaries.

"Going alone among strangers, though treated kindly, she has had to encounter many obstacles which she has bravely faced. In recognition of her courage and public spirit, it is desired to raise a sum which will pay her tuition fees, and relieve her from pecuniary anxiety during her absence.

"Mr. James, No. 2 Camoe Street, Calcutta, will be happy to receive subscriptions.

Subscriptions.

	Rupees.
His Excellency the Viceroy and Governor-General .	200
His Honor the Lieut.-Governor	100
The Honorable Chief-Justice Garth	50
The Hon. J. Gibbs, C. S. I., C. I. E.	100
The Hon. C. I. Albert, C. I. E.	50
The Hon. Mr. Justice Pigot	50
Mr. James	200
	750

It was this money, with whatever was subsequently added to it, that Mrs. Joshee refers to as the "James fund."

She often complains now of taking cold.

Mr. Sattay, a friend of Gopal's, came from India in November, bringing with him bright sarees and embroidered jackets for Anandabai. It was delightful to her to hear the familiar rippling cadences of the Mahratta tongue once more.

In December, 1884, she came to Washington and made what we both intended should have been the first of many visits to me. The final decline of her health, and the circumstances of her last year in this country, interfered. This visit was the only one.

I had seen her for the first time shortly after her arrival in Philadelphia, on the 6th of October, 1883. In my diary for that day I find the following entry connected with various items of information already communicated in these pages: —

"I had promised to pass the evening at Dr. Bodley's, that I might meet the young Mahratta woman, who has come here to study medicine. As I had a high opinion of the intelligence of her tribe, I was surprised to find that a 'nose-ring' formed part of her costume although she wisely refrains from wearing it. Certainly, I never heard it spoken of in connection with Bengali women. She insists on wearing her native dress, and although she wore three necklaces, three pairs of earrings, her nose-ring as a brooch, six pairs of bangles, and a saree of crimson and gold, at the reception held for her by Dr. Bodley, she was so plainly dressed to-night that she would have attracted no attention in the street, provided she had worn a bonnet. She was however so ill that I ought not to judge her. She looks like a stout dumpy mulatto girl not especially interesting until her yellow face lights up, and light up it did as soon as she gathered from a helping word of mine, that I was familiar with the customs of her people. I cannot describe the effect. It was magical. She speaks seven languages, of which English, Sanscrit and Mahratta are three. Her English is exquisite. There is hardly a flaw in pronunciation or construction. If I had not known, I should have thought her born in this country. She has not a single 'cockney' trick of speech.

"She has none of the delicate features which distinguish the Bengalis.

"Her feeling of caste is still uppermost. She receives her guests with impassive dignity like a true Oriental, and was one of only two or three in her class who chose to stay and see a painful operation for necrosis performed on a young child this week. It was not from indifference, for she spoke of it with painful emotion. She has *shown* curiosity but once, however much she may have felt it. Among those invited to meet her was a mulatto lady, who took a medical degree two or three years ago, and is highly esteemed in Philadelphia. Anandabai looked her all over and evidently did not make her out. There was nothing to show her that the mulatto was not a Hindu except the European dress.

"I was much interested in my conversation with this woman, however disappointed I felt as to her personal attractions. She had a blue tattooed mark between her eyes, a little like an anchor. She told me that this was inserted soon after birth, that she might be recognized as a Hindu, not mistaken for a Mahometan. Sometimes she thought family marks were made in the same way. The scarlet spot of paste which she wore on her forehead must be put on fresh every morning, by every married woman, as a sign that she is married, and the marriage vows must be silently repeated when it is laid on. Certainly, there are married women in this country who might well follow the fashion!

"When we parted, she put out her hand. 'I feel as if I had found a friend,' she said. 'It is the first time anybody has known about me,' and then I saw beauty in the lambent eyes."

As time went on, I grew familiar with what had at first disappointed me, and saw the fascinations of movement and manner that others felt so deeply. It was the Oriental charm, but I do not think that in her own country she would ever have been called handsome. Her motions were sinuous, not serpentine like those of the Bengalis. Her beautiful hands and feet, her elastic muscles belonged to her race rather than herself. In one respect from first to last, she was herself alone, in the sweetest truthfulness, the most entire candor, that ever belonged to a mortal, and I have good reason to think that this is not a common Hindu trait.

Mrs. Carpenter thought her very beautiful, but not at first. The thought came upon her suddenly, when Mrs. Joshee came down one morning dressed for church, and radiant with her own holy thoughts.

In her conversation with me, Anandabai talked about the Theosophists and the Brahmos, and if she had not distinctly said in her address at Serampore, that she was not a Brahmo, I should have supposed her to be one, so much sympathy did she show with their movement. I saw her once more and wrote to her and heard from her several times before, on the 26th of Dec. 1884, I went to the cars to bring her to my Georgetown house. Everything about her arrival was unfortunate. The cars were so late that the carriage

I had engaged was gone, and the demand on their arrival so great, that having no escort it was impossible for me to secure another. We were obliged to go out in a horse-car, and this was not desirable on account of the attention she could not fail to attract. Beside this, she had some heavy hand baggage which she would not let me carry up the hill. I remarked with surprise the calmness with which she endured the curious gaze of our companions, and the courage with which she bore her burden and encountered the necessary fatigues. She was a striking contrast to the English ladies who came over to Philadelphia with the British Association that same year. During her stay with me I took her to all the public buildings, to a service at the Unitarian church, to several private lunches, to dine with Commodore Walker's family and two other friends, and to several receptions. Nowhere did any peculiar awkwardness draw any attention to her foreign education.

It pleased her to steal quietly about my house, taking up and touching the various articles that had been sent from India.

On the 29th of December, I wrote in my Journal: —

"A very unpleasant day, but we had fifty-two callers, and in the evening gave a light supper to thirty.

Last evening Mrs. Joshee talked well, about the antiquity of her nation, and of her family record, which she asserts is two thousand years old. She promises to write me details about it, and to send me some of the peculiar paper upon which it is written, when she returns home. To-night, before quite a large company, she talked in an earnest and excited way about the religions of the world, showing a profound intelligence as well as scholarship. Then for a while in a very entertaining way about jewels and costumes. Her best talk was with the Rev. Theodore Wynkoop, after most of our friends had gone.

"To-night she wore a close satin vest embroidered with gold, and a white camel's hair shawl or saree deeply bordered with gold; also her collars and necklaces of jewels, and for the first time, at my request, her 'nose-ring.' This is a spray of flowers two or three inches long, and made of fine old pearls. The pearls were some of those given by the king to her warlike ancestor in Poonah. The centres of the starlike flowers are of ruby and emerald. A fine wire attaches it to the left nostril close to the cheek. It is very effective, much prettier than ear-rings, and looks as if she were holding a spray of flowers between her lips."

We went some days after to see Major Powell, and arranged for some specimens of North American pottery which Anandabai wanted to carry to

India and promised to replace by specimens from Poonah. After a visit to the White House, I spent one evening in taking notes of her conversation. Very much longer should I have written had I guessed for a moment that it would be my last opportunity.

Previous to Anandabai's arrival in this country, a letter of her writing was sent to a psychometrist in New York. The following "impression" derived from this letter, and dated January 20th, 1881, nearly a year and a half before any American had seen her, has been copied into a Calcutta paper, and sent to me since I began to write these pages. It seems to me so just an estimate of her character, that I value it exactly as I value the "impressions" of John Quincy Adams and Daniel Webster, written out by my friend Anna Parsons more than thirty years ago.

"This is an intellectual well-balanced mind, cultivated with great care," the paper begins. "The writer is a lady of more than ordinary brain power, very independent, but neither egotistical nor intolerant. She is not afraid to investigate any subject however unpopular. She is analytical and very frank in speaking her mind. She converses fluently and meets strangers with a cordial, graceful ease that wins confidence and esteem. She has talent as an instructor, a clear style of expression easy to be understood. She has great equanimity, enjoys the attention of refined people, and naturally drifts into the society of the best, but never shrinks from those less fortunate if she can do them good. She has a taste for missionary work, and an executiveness and systematic way of managing that are quite original. She has great delicacy of character, is womanly in every respect, has an ardent love of nature and clings to old friends and associations and to family ties. Her radicalism springs from a holy desire to do her duty. She has a religious cast of mind, is very spiritual but seems to know nothing of *spiritualism.* Her penetrative mind is constantly reaching for more light. She perceives the character of others readily and is seldom deceived, has a fine memory and good descriptive powers. In travelling nothing escapes her.

"I see her in the future as one who has no superior; living for truth, justice, and honor. She will always defend the weak. She has great forbearance, is seldom offended, and when she is, it passes and leaves no cloud upon her brow. She has a large *hope* which will sustain her as long as she lives."

Since I began to write this Life, I have met a gentleman who listened to Anandabai's talk at my house on the evening to which I have alluded. I asked him if he had preserved any record of that brilliant conversation. "No," he said thoughtfully, "I cannot report anything that she said, but I remember wondering when I realized how soon the foreigner and the lion I went to see, was lost in the sweet and cultivated woman with whom it was a pleasure to talk."

During that year Anandabai made a convert. She was invited to tea one evening by a young physician who seemed to think that she should please her guest by a sort of agnostic conversation, expressing utter scepticism as to the existence of a Supreme Being, which was on the contrary very painful. Anandabai sat quietly through the meal, but when it was over, she asked her hostess to withdraw with her. As soon as they reached a chamber, she placed the astonished girl in a chair, and kneeling down beside her, entreated God to take pity on her and send her light.

The consequences of this interview were remarkable. Some time after, Anandabai writes of her: "She used to laugh at every one who believed in God. There is no more satirical speech. She invited me to tea. After supper I was surprised to see her sit piously with folded hands and invite me to do the same. What a change!"

How little had it ever entered into the head of our dear friend, when she prepared for coming to

America, that she would ever be called to a duty like this! Yet she had, as the psychometrist said, the heart of a missionary in her.

During this year she made several excursions into different parts of Pennsylvania and delivered an address to the students of the College at Bordentown, New Jersey.

Mr. Joshee arrived from India during the summer of 1885. The first notice of his coming was received through California newspapers which were sent to his wife's dearest friends. How strangely small this world appears when we reflect that wherever we travel, we cannot escape those who are on the watch for our misdeeds! In this paper, Mr. Joshee was reported as having made an address unfriendly to the higher education of women. "This unfitted them," he asserted, "for the domestic duties of wives and mothers." A voice from the crowd shouted, "I thought your own wife was studying medicine in Philadelphia?" "Oh, yes!" said Mr. Joshee, and then he shrugged his shoulders and spread out his hands, as if he would say, "How could I help that?" When I received this paper I sent it at once to Philadelphia, with the inquiries it suggested. All our friends were troubled. No one seemed to know whether Anandabai had received the news, but the moment we met in the autumn I knew that she had seen the paper. A change had passed over her as subtle as that the hoar-frost breathes over the summer grass. She met her husband at Roselle and in that summer — the summer of 1885 — she went with him to Greenwood, and to hear Talmage and Ward Beecher in Brooklyn. Mr. Joshee went alone to Washington. Of course, he did not find me there, but he went to my house, and there encountered the lady who had charge of it in my absence. More ignorant than the rest of us of various embarrassing complications, this lady, who had been greatly attracted to his wife, looked at him sharply and said, "Was it you, then, who made that speech in San Francisco?" "Yes," replied Gopal. "And what did you do it for?" she persisted. "Just for a little fun," was the answer. "I thought I would stir them up a little."

Mr. Joshee could have had a very inadequate idea of the interest Anandabai had aroused in this country, and he could have understood very little the character of his wife, if he expected her to be pleased by fun of that sort. I have recorded his reply, because I never gratified him by any inquiries concerning the matter, nor am I aware that any of his wife's friends ever did so. Anandabai spent her Christmas vacation at Roselle, and as she was to graduate in March, she devoted much of this time to the preparation of her graduation "Thesis" on "Hindu Obstetrics."

After the fifty pages were finished and submitted, she wrote as follows to Mrs. Carpenter:

PHILADELPHIA, Jan. 31st, 1886.

MY DEAR AUNT, — Your disappointment in my change of plan is not greater than mine. I had planned for four months ahead, from March. I had forty and one things to finish or accomplish before my Hospital service began. But things rotated, no doubt; for our best. I found I must enter the New England hospital next May. You know I have given up Blockley entirely, but will try the competitive for the Woman's Hospital for six months. The friends and authorities of the New England Hospital are very kind to me. They have made special arrangement for me to go there for six months, which is not generally allowable at all. Beside, my application went too late, all the places were filled, yet they are so anxious to help me, that they are going to accept me as an extra student or interne. Such students pay board, but they make me their guest. Dr. Tyng is also willing to take me for six months provided I pass the competitive. Now everything depends on my graduating. If faithful attendance and diligent study with some practical knowledge deserve any reward at all, I have no reason to fear next March, but I have to wait for it.

Do not buy me anything for my graduation. Your presence will make me more happy than any gift. It is not as if I had no memento; but nothing can be added. If you were troubled with wealth, I would accept anything you might present me. Now I hope you will present yourselves, which is the richest of gifts.

I had the misfortune to fall on the ice and break all the bangles on my right arm. My husband bought me a gold bracelet, as I could not go without anything. If every fall would bring as much gold, would you consider it a misfortune? I called it so, because the money might have bought me an instrument that would have been useful or a book that would have been instructive. I got another present as a graduating student, five weeks in advance. It is a beautiful gold watch. It was given me by a wealthy lady, whom you will probably see in March.

Our theses, ticket money, and application for degree were sent in last week. I do not yet know whether my "Thesis" is accepted. There were fifty pages of it, just fitting, so that not another word could have gone in; the longest one they had.

It is quite evident that Anandabai was still so completely a Hindu that she considered her bangles as necessary as her saree. I thought I saw a great change in her, when we met this year in October. Not only was she more delicate in health, but she seemed to have lost courage. It is certain that she did not take and could never afterward resume the place she had easily held for the last two years in the College Classes. If her graduation had depended upon this last year, she could not have taken her degree. Her condition will perhaps explain the following letter, written Feb. 8th, 1886:—

"Love and duty are sacred and *my own.* I can always love, although I cannot always expect to be loved. So I can always perform my own duty, although I may not persuade others to theirs. I do not do this for the promise of any earthly pleasure nor even for those termed Heavenly, but for simple duty's sake. Heaven, if it be only a place of indulgence and banqueting, would have no charm for me, for these might disappear and leave me paralyzed and idle. It is always well to look into the future just far enough to guide our steps and prepare for any immediate obstruction, but I think it is foolish, if not worse, to mourn over the possible future when the present needs all our watchfulness and strength. My physical self is like the days of September, and my brain and nerves seem 'dissected up' like the warp on the loom, distinct and bare, but sensitive."

She was very unwell, dreading a fresh attack of diphtheria, which was however averted. A few days later she writes to Mrs. Carpenter: —

PHILADELPHIA, March 7th, 1886.

DEAR AUNT, — After all I am able to sit down at my ease and write to my dear ones. I am through the studies so far as college life is concerned, but, oh dear! there is more that comes after than goes before.

Results received yesterday and I am passed. I am thankful, for my patience was almost worn out. On the last question of the last paper I broke down, and could not even see whether I finished my sentence. I pinned the papers together and left the room without even bowing to the Professor. Our Japanese friend did very well. The Syrian student, after most wonderful and formidable attacks of diseases and rewarding her benefactors and well-wishers with her ingratitude, was made to leave us. Her condition is sadder than death, if death is at all sad. She brought tears of pity to my eyes, — eyes that had so far had no occasion to shed tears of such pity or disgust. We were all miserable on her account.

Pundita Ramabai arrived safely. The storm and low water detained her in the river. I spent two full days on the wharf waiting for her. Her child is here, a little darling. She is as bright as sunshine and as sweet as a fresh rosebud. She must give a great deal of comfort to her mother, who has passed through too many sorrows for one woman. She was brought up and petted by sensitive and loving hearts. She is a woman, tender with feeling, as tender as a flower, timid as can be and impatient of pain, but her courage has outweighed that of the sternest and bravest warrior. She has filled my heart with a real joy. I hope you will like her when you see her. I began to write this letter yesterday, but so much else came in the way! I went to my Examination at the College at 7.45 this morning, and came home at 2.40 P. M. The examination was very long and tedious, though it could not be considered *hard*. I did not have much sleep last night and I was very tired; am so tired I can hardly keep my eyes open or my hand under control. I am so glad you are going to stay a day longer for the lecture of Rama Bai.

This letter shows how evenly balanced were all my dear friend's faculties and powers. Her brain acted only in the service of her heart.

Mrs. Carpenter thinks that the few days covered by this letter were the most trying to body and brain that Anandabai passed in this country. The exposure on the wharf was a very serious thing for one as exhausted as she was by the College work; but her heart was so warm that she thought far less of the result for which she had toiled so earnestly for three whole years, than of welcoming the devoted and lovely kinswoman whom she had never seen.

She had never seen her, but this was by no means the first time Anandabai had shown her gifted cousin a warm sympathy and regard. When Ramabai was left a widow, and the Joshees knew that her independent and vigorous career had created an opposition likely to molest her, a warm invitation was sent by Anandabai offering a home in her own house to the desolate widow. Ramabai was not able to accept the invitation, but from that time the strength of a common purpose — the determination to elevate the women of their native land — sustained the correspondence which had then begun.

On the 10th of March, 1886, I went to Philadelphia to remain a day or two with Anandabai, to make the acquaintance of the Pundita, and to be present at the varied exercises of the week. I wrote in my Journal that night: —

"I have seen Anandabai, Ramabai and her child. Ramabai is strikingly beautiful. Her face is a clean-cut oval; her eyes, dark and large, glow with feeling. She is a brunette, but her cheeks are full of color. Her white widow's saree is drawn closely over her head and fastened under her chin. There is nothing else about her to suggest the Hindu. I cross-questioned Anandabai pretty closely about a possible mixture of blood. She acknowledged that there is a frequent crossing of the Mahratta blood by that of Cashmere."

At noon, on the 11th of March, I went to the Green Room of the Academy of Music, where the Graduation Exercises were to be held. It was full of bright young girls and flowers. When we went out upon the stage we confronted an audience of three thousand persons.

Anandabai, the Pundita and her pretty little child were seated near enough to the front of the stage to be distinctly visible to the audience. It was a far more memorable day than any of that audience knew.

Anandabai and her kinswoman had sailed from India in the same month: Anandabai from Calcutta to New York; Ramabai from Bombay to the sisters at Wantage in England, where she embraced Christianity in 1883.

On the day Anandabai left Liverpool for New York, Ramabai landed in England. These two women were cousins three times removed, but the same courage, the same aspirations animated both. Ramabai was the child of Ananta Shastri and his second wife, Lakshmibai. Ananta had determined to educate his first wife, but was prevented by the bigotry and prejudice of his family and her own. She died early, and, when the same obstacles to education presented themselves to oppress his second wife, Ananta withdrew from the world and made his home in the wilderness. Ramabai was the youngest of his children; she grew up unfettered in the outer world. It is touching to hear her tell how her mother taught her Sanscrit in the early morning of each day, waking her with caresses and making her very lullabies a lesson in language. Ananta spent his large property before Ramabai was grown, and spent it chiefly in efforts to stimulate the education of Hindu women. After the death of her father, she and her only surviving brother travelled through the country, advocating their father's views. At Calcutta the pundits received her. A Professor tested her knowledge of Sanscrit and the honorary title of "Sarasvati" was conferred upon her. Sarasvati is the name of the Goddess of Arts and Learning.

Married and left a widow with one child, she determined like Anandabai to devote her life to the elevation of her own sex. In England, she became a Christian. When I asked her why she had allowed herself to be baptized she replied, "The Shasters contain all the principles of a religious life, but they offer us no example of it. In Jesus I have the word made flesh. But I do not belong to the church of England nor to any other church. I told them it must be so, when they baptized me. I believe in the Bible, but I will believe in it in my own way."

Before her departure from India, Ramabai had founded a society in Poonah to aid in the establishment of native schools for girls, and travelled throughout the Bombay Presidency to form branch societies. When the English Educational Commission visited Poonah in September, 1882, Ramabai met them in the town hall, with more than three hundred Mahratta women and children, and welcomed them with an address in English. So impressed was Dr. Hunter, the President of that Commission, with the earnestness of these women, that he had Ramabai's testimony before it translated into English. Her plea for the medical education of the native women gave a needed impetus to the Countess of Dufferin's movement, — a movement which owed much more, however, to the excitement produced in India by Anandabai's address at Serampore and subsequent departure for America.

At Wantage, Ramabai perfected her knowledge of the English language, and in 1884 she went to the Ladies' College at Cheltenham as Professor of Sanscrit. We had heard much of these two women, and now they sat modestly before the immense audience that thronged the Academy. How different they were! One so strikingly beautiful that she arrested every eye, the other self-absorbed, unconscious, with her gaze fixed upon the Highest. One impulsive, practical, bent on carrying out certain plans for the benefit of her people; the other devout, self-controlled, thinking first of all of the great mysteries of life and work.

I quote again from my Journal:—

"Mrs. Joshee wore a pure white saree richly bordered with gold. Although not in the least beautiful, she is the sweetest impersonation of pure womanliness that I have ever seen. All eyes were on her. Ramabai, who wears the plain white 'Chudda' of the Mahratta widow, has a really handsome face, a delicate skin flushed with brilliant color. She and her little girl look like Spaniards. Neither is graceful, while every motion of Anandabai gives pleasure. An immense quantity of flowers was distributed at the close of Dr. Marshall's address, and Anandabai had many valuable presents, books, instruments and money, to help her carry out her purposes. She could hardly be insensible to the fact that she was the observed of all observers; she must have heard the frequent and honorable mention of her name, nor could she have been deaf to the applause of that immense audience when she went forward to take her Diploma, but not even the quiver of her lips betrayed her."

There was not a vacant seat in the Academy when the exercises began. People stood against the walls and under the galleries, sat upon the steps, and filled every aisle and doorway. The students of the College filled the front seats in the pit, and the Faculty with their invited guests crowded the stage.

A mass of flowers in baskets, bouquets and varied designs, covered the footlights and completely hid the piles of costly gifts, to be presented by friends of the students to the graduates after the Diplomas were given out.

The next evening Ramabai gave her first address in America, on the subject which fills all her thoughts. For an hour before this began, we received in an ante-room about eighty ladies of the highest social position, whom Dr. Bodley wished to introduce to her Indian friends. The audience in the Hall itself was estimated at from five to six hundred. Ramabai spoke as Anandabai does, as if English were her native tongue, but there is a certain piquancy and originality in all that

Anandabai says, not to be found elsewhere. The audience was reverent, struck by the speaker's beauty and awed by her enthusiasm and eloquence. Never shall I forget the hush which followed her appeal when, after clasping her hands in silence for a few moments, she lifted her voice to God in earnest entreaty for her countrywomen. The whole city echoed the next day with wondering inquiry and explanation.

A day or two after, the Joshees and the Pundita were received by the Century Club, and this entertainment was followed by invitations of many kinds to many places in and out of town.

I had never seen Gopal Joshee, until I went to Philadelphia, on this memorable week, but I had heard of his visit to my own house, and observed the manner in which he bore himself toward his wife's best friends. During this visit prolonged for some days, after Anandabai had taken her diploma, I saw less of her than I desired, I was so anxious to possess myself of a fair and candid opinion of this strange man. After the first courtesies when we met, he was so absolutely silent for some days in my presence, that my friends thought I must have offended him. After this, he talked very freely before me but not to me, and I only knew that he was conscious of my existence, by the readiness with which he aided me when I wanted copies of the leading papers or any special information. It is with great pain that I speak of him for Anandabai loved him, but it is impossible to write her life truly, without suggesting the "tangle" which his presence brought into her daily life.

Anandabai had been most generously and delicately aided by the ladies of Philadelphia, and this aid it was easy for them to render because she accepted it for her people and her work. While awaiting her husband's coming, she had no idea, that instead of asking for a few months' leave, he would be obliged to throw up the work by which they had hitherto lived. When I asked her why he had done so, she said briefly and with a deep sigh "He is tired," but would not pursue the subject. After his coming, he shared the generous and provident kindness which had been extended to her, but he received it differently and she knew it.

In Dr. Bodley's Preface to the "High Caste Hindu Woman," a book written by Ramabai, she says of Dr. Joshee, —

"Ramabai's chapter on the married life of the Hindu woman reveals to the Western Reader what it was for this refined, intellectual person, whose faculties developed rapidly under Western opportunities, and whose scientific acquirements placed her high in rank among her peers in the college class, to accept again the position awarded her by the Code of Manu. That she did accept it, that 'until death she was patient of hardships, self-controlled, and strove to fulfil that most excellent duty prescribed for wives,' is undoubted. Let those who recognize this herculean attempt find in it a clue to the influences which dealt the final fatal blow."

In a letter written by Gopal to one of his friends in this country, during the distracted days that followed his wife's death in Poonah, he says, "I wonder if she would not be living still, if I had never gone to America?"

Strange that he should have written this, and stranger still would he have deemed it, had he known that the one thought that rang through my brain, as we sat together day after day in Philadelphia was this: "He will make life impossible to her."

This year presented peculiar causes for anxiety, and for Mr. Joshee's excitability, dissatisfaction and restlessness there is some excuse to be found in the condition of his wife's health, and the impossibility of tempting her appetite with suitable food wherever she might be. Gopal had entered the United States by the wrong gate. The restless life of the West, the disorganizations of the border, did not give him the key he needed to understand the Eastern States. He saw very little, but thought he saw everything. This however he did perceive, that Anandabai's health was failing, and unable to aid her himself, half frantic with affection and anxiety, he required of us all what it was impossible to give. Little did he know that it was chiefly owing to Dr. Bodley's tender foresight, that his wife was still living. To provide her with an abundance of nutritious vegetable food was often impossible, and there was not a physician anywhere who would not have said she needed broth and delicate meats; but these she could not take.

It was probably in one of the fits of irritation produced by circumstances that he had not been in the country long enough to understand, that Gopal wrote a letter to "The Index," on the 14th of March, 1886. This letter concerned "child marriage," a subject brought into most unhappy prominence by the discussion of the story of Rukhmabai, a young Brahmin lady who, betrothed to a worthless and aged husband in childhood, refused to consummate the abominable contract, and was sent to prison in consequence. Gopal's letter insanely denies the plain facts of this case, with which all Europe was already familiar. In it he makes assertions which he knew were not true, and assumes a position in regard to the American people which must have given sharp pain to his gentle wife. While arrogance and assumption breathe in every line of his letter, he coolly demands that Americans shall "say no word against *his* country!" All this was written at a moment when he listened daily to the sad exposition which Ramabai was offering to the public.

Any one who will turn to "The Index" for April 1st, 1886, will be astonished at the forbearance of its Editor. In an article published by Max Müller in the London Times of Aug. 22nd, 1887, the interested reader may prove to himself how utterly unreliable were Mr. Joshee's statements.

Whoever had walked the streets of Philadelphia in modest peace with Anandabai, could not fail to find a difference when Gopal was added to the party.

His excited manner, his loud and rapid talk attracted the attention of the crowd, and this was held by the floating blue wrap, the white scarf, and dark turban which he always wore.

About this time the beautiful dress worn by

Anandabai on the day of her graduation became the theme of public discussion, and as it was necessary to correct various errors concerning it, the following account was sent to the local papers: —

"The friends of Dr. Anandabai Joshee who are accustomed to associate a simple and childlike sincerity with everything relating to her, were at first amused and then a little pained, when several of the daily papers spoke of her receiving her degree in a robe 'trimmed with tinsel!'

"There was no more 'tinsel' on her robe than there is in her character. The snowy gold-bordered dress she wore, was part of her wedding outfit, made to her father's order. It was made in the old city of Chunder, famous through many centuries for the production of the finest hand-made India mull. This long narrow garment is the usual saree or upper garment of the Mahratta women, but Anandabai does not wear it in the usual way. The Pundits found the fashion among the dresses worn by her ancestors when they dwelt on snow-covered hills. This garment is made of a kind of India muslin called 'chally.'

"This word, like our word 'shawl,' is derived from the name of King Shawliwan, in whose reign and at whose desire shawls were first made eighteen hundred years ago.

"This muslin saree is four yards long and two and

a half wide. The gold border is four inches wide round the bottom, and more than nine up and down the front. Beside the wide stripe there are two narrow ones; and these borders are not even made of gold thread, but of flat drawn gold so pure that it washes like a gold ring. This border is so very heavy that no machine-made goods would hold it. It is equally perfect and beautiful on the two sides. No one who has seen the saree daintily worn can fail to be charmed with it, and I need hardly point out to those who have seen the Tanagra statuettes, that in many cases it is the saree which imparts the peculiar charm to the Greek figurine."

Probably nothing in her life was so trying to Dr. Joshee as the round of visits which now began in her husband's company. She could not escape from the group of friends who listened while he poured out in his rapid impulsive way his bitter complaint against the country and people which she so dearly loved. Alone I had known her more than once to interpose her gentle word, but before others her duty as a Hindu wife forbade her to speak. Her silence seemed to strangers like sullenness. Gopal had been accustomed to this in her younger days, and it did not affect him as it did those who had seen her in her happy freedom before his arrival. It had one serious result, however; those who saw her for the first time after her husband reached Philadelphia, especially those who met her first in Massachusetts, never saw the delightful and fascinating woman so beloved by her friends in Philadelphia.

On the 16th of April Dr. Joshee left Roselle for Philadelphia, intending to be examined for Blockley Hospital. She expected to pass the summer at the "New England Hospital for Women and Children," and to enter Blockley for practice the following winter.

But her plans were very suddenly changed. Dr. Bodley had been asked to supply a resident physician to the female wards of the new Albert Edward Hospital at Kolhapur, and about this time the following letter was received:—

To DR. RACHEL BODLEY,
Woman's Medical College, Philadelphia, Pa.

KOLHAPUR, March 10th, 1886.

DEAR MADAM,—I beg you will kindly excuse me for not replying to your letter of Nov. 25th before. After I wrote you my first letter, the fact that Dr. Anandabai Joshee would appear for her final examination at your College in the current month, was brought to my notice by the Hon. Rao Bahadur

M. G. Ranadè. Thinking that nothing could be more desirable than to have a native of India for our "Lady Doctor," I placed myself at once in communication with my friend, that he might ascertain from Mrs. Joshee whether she would accept the appointment alluded to. I hear that she is willing.

I beg therefore that you will do me the favor to offer the place to Mrs. Joshee on the following terms.

1. Mrs. Joshee's designation to be Lady Doctor of Kolhapur.

2. Her salary per month to be Rs. 300 at first, to be increased to 400 after two years' service, and to 500 after five years'.

3. A house for habitation with ordinary furniture to be provided, but this not to include service or board.

4. The expenses of a single passage from the United States to India will be borne by the State of Kolhapur, on condition that this be refunded in the event of Mrs. Joshee's leaving the service in less than one year.

5. The engagement shall be for seven years, but may be terminated by either party on giving six months' notice.

6. Mrs. Joshee will be in charge of the Albert Edward Hospital, subject to the general supervision of the Durbar Doctor, and instruct a class of girls in medicine, etc.

7. Private practice will be allowed to any extent that will not interfere with public duties, but no fees are to be charged for attending on the ladies of the palace, or on the wives of contributors to the Hospital Funds.

I assure you that the supervision of the Durbar Doctor will be friendly. I feel sure that Doctor Sinclair, our Durbar Surgeon, and Doctor Joshee will pull well together.

Mrs. Joshee seems to think that we mean our pupils to be nurses only. Our object is much higher,—to enable them to be general practitioners.

When the Bombay scheme for Female Medical Education, which has been taken in hand by Lady Reay, the wife of our Governor, has been perfected, it is our intention to have the Kolhapur Establishment affiliated to the Central College. Close to Mrs. Joshee's quarters will be provided quarters for the pupils, that they may be under her constant supervision.

In conclusion, I have to request that you will communicate the wishes of Mrs. Joshee by the return mail. If she accepts, I shall want a letter from her to that effect, stating also whether she can be at the Hospital by the first of June.

Thanking you heartily for your prompt reply to my first letter and for your offer of assistance,

I remain yours sincerely,

MEHERJE COOVERJE,

The Dewan of Kolhapur.

I am sorry to say that I have no copy of Dr. Joshee's reply to this letter, which was written on the 18th of April, but one remarkable sentence in it is impressed upon my memory.

After a cordial acceptance of the appointment Anandabai went on to say:—

"There is nothing in the seven conditions which you name, that causes me any uneasiness, but if any question were likely to arise under it, I might object to the seventh.

"Our Shasters require us to impart the gifts of healing and of religious truth without pay, and to this practice I shall adhere; but if I ever meant to take a fee from any one, it would assuredly be from those who are rich and powerful, and never from those who are poor and depressed."

On the 12th of June, 1886, the Dewan of Kolhapur, an officer of the government corresponding to our Secretary of State, acknowledged Dr. Joshee's acceptance of the position in the Albert Edward Hospital, and consented to allow her to spend the summer in Roxbury as she desired.

She intended to sail in January, 1887.

It was about this time that I began to feel very anxious about Anandabai's health. The climate of the United States at its best seems fatal to the Asiatic. The Aleut fares no better than the

Hindu on these shores, and when disease attacks either, it is astonishing how quickly the end comes. The climate of Cutch and of Calcutta had been very injurious to Dr. Joshee's health, and she was depressed by unnatural lassitude when she reached Philadelphia. The home of her dearest friend, which speedily became her home also, was in Roselle, in a part of New Jersey subject to malarial and depressing influences. If we had had an examination in 1883, the lesson of her life would have been lost. The one thing that might have saved her was a long and steady residence in Colorado or New Mexico, with a light heart. It was because she was so happy the first two years that we were deceived as to her health. As soon as she had accepted the position at Kolhapur, her whole future weighed upon her. Assuming by virtue of her larger earnings the duties of the head of her family, she had to look forward, not only to supporting herself and performing her duties at the Hospital, but upon her would fall the care of her husband's mother and younger brothers. Her first duty on her return would be to go to Nassik, where they resided, and complete arrangements for their removal to Kolhapur. At this time she supposed she should be well enough to go to India alone, and it was thought that Mr. Joshee might remain for some time in England and America. I have said that she was to have the care of her husband's family, but what sort of influence were they to exert over her? She had said, "I will go to America as a Hindu, and I will remain a Hindu. I will be in all things *his* deserving wife." What says the Shaster?

"For the ancient sages declare that a bride is given to the family of her husband and not to her husband alone." (Apastamba, 2nd, 10th, 27th, 3d.)

And again in the IXth of Manu, 22nd, we read:

"Whatever be the qualities of the man with whom a woman is united in lawful marriage, such qualities she must assume, as a river mingles with the ocean."

Could she indeed remain his "deserving wife"? Was this any longer possible to her? No word escaped her lips. Obediently she stooped to lift her heavy burden; but those who loved her, felt her heart sinking, although her words were the words of cheerful courage.

To the New England Hospital she went as an invited guest on the 2nd of May. She would have "ample opportunity," she was told, "to visit other infirmaries and asylums not unfriendly to women." Such an arrangement, it was said, "would give no opportunity for the care and responsibility devolving upon an *interne*, but would give her the chance to see a great variety of work."

What she actually encountered the following letter will show. It was something wholly unsuited to the delicate condition which her friends hardly suspected, and of which the authorities at the Hospital could not be aware.

ROXBURY, May 3d, 1886.

MY DEAR AUNT, — I reached here last evening at about 7 o'clock. Two of my college friends came very kindly to meet me, so that made it pleasant all through. I have already taken charge of the medical ward here. I went to the Maternity to see a case, soon after I arrived, before supper. This morning at seven I visited the medical ward. At 8.30 I went with another Interne to the Surgical. I paid another visit at 12.30 with Dr. P. This is one of the regular visits.

I have to visit my own ward again this evening, so you see how busy I am! I have to make three regular visits beside that with Dr. P. to all the Hospital, after which the consulting physician, resident physician and the Internes meet in the office to discuss the cases. My sleeping-room is on the third floor, dining-room on the lowest, patients all over. I have to fill up the papers that belong to my own patients. This is the first time I have sat down. I am so tired!

The spot in which the Hospital stands is one of the most delightful that I have seen. It is perfectly charming. It was so cold in the house, that I came out on the lawn to write. It is very sunny, but very windy, so I don't think I shall stay long.

When I read those words, I thought I knew when the final blow was struck. Was there no one to warn her? Exhausted, chilled, she needed as much warmth as a tropical bird, and she went out of doors to write on the 3d of May, in a Boston east wind! She goes on:—

Will you please give the Roorhacks my address, and tell them not to send me the knife for wood carving or anything else. I have to be moving from room to room and place to place, and have no time for anything. After all, I have regular duty to perform. One of my college friends has left the Hospital entirely, the other is miles off in the Dispensary.

You will be sorry to hear that I have such a cold in my throat that I cannot talk, only whisper. There is measles in the Annex, so one *Interne* must stay there. Two others have left. Dr. Hall is here, but Dr. Sterling has not yet come. With love, your

ANANDABAI.

The letters that followed recorded days equally crowded with work, although occasionally varied with pleasant change. She went to a tea at the Woman's Club, to the Woman's Industrial Union, and took many drives with Dr. Keller to see some of her most interesting surgical cases. Writing of Boston, she says, "I am so impressed with the beauty of Boston! I am ready to say it is the prettiest place I have seen in America." No one seems to have seen how ill she was, and oh, I know without asking, that through all this time no one saw the real Anandabai! It must have been in the early part of her stay that she received a visit from Mrs. Underwood. Mrs. Underwood went to invite her to deliver an address at the coming anniversary of the Free Religious Association, in which she should explain her own position and the needs of women in India. "There entered," writes Mrs. Underwood, "a graceful, childlike creature, the lustrous eyes of whose dark grave face sought those of her visitor in quiet scrutiny." Dr. Joshee declined this invitation on the ground of her duties at the Hospital.

My mind had been a little withdrawn from her at this time by changes in my own life. I did not hear from my friend as I expected, till on the first of June Mr. Joshee wrote to Mrs. Carpenter that his wife had decided to give up her studies at the Hospital, and see if perfect rest would not prepare her for her duties at Kolhapur. I was hurrying North at the moment, and reached the Hospital on the morning of June 5th, only to be shocked at the announcement that Mrs. Joshee was confined to her room. I found her lying in bed, pale and quiet. As we sat hand in hand looking into each other's eyes for a long while, I thought with satisfaction how lately she had said, "I have no need of words. I know what my friends think without words." There were many questions that I wished to ask, but she was in no condition to talk. To my surprise, she did not seem anxious about herself, but was incommoded by some internal difficulty brought on by the constant going up and down stairs, which the Hospital Service required. What little talk we had was about Ramabai and her plans. Dr. Joshee was expecting to work with her in India. She was grieved to give up her Hospital Work, but intended to go that afternoon to visit Dr. Keller, and from thence by short stages, making visits at Providence and Hartford, to Roselle. I think she was not able to move till the 9th of June, and it was perhaps while she was resting peacefully at Dr. Keller's that she rallied enough to go to Mrs. Underwood for an evening, and meet a few friends.

Of this meeting Mrs. Underwood wrote as follows: —

"She wore no bonnet, but instead a fawn-colored wrap enveloped her finely shaped head and gracefully draped her shoulders; this was removed on entering. Her robe of some fine dark woollen material was edged to the depth of several inches with gold-colored embroidery, and in spite of its flowing drapery at one arm, fitted nicely her plump *petite* form; gold bracelets adorned her wrists. The dark face was round, with full lips; she had a handsomely shaped brow, broad and intellectual looking. Between the eyebrows was a small tattooed mark, in shape somewhat like a cross. The eyes were beautiful and expressive, large, black, softly shining, as capable of smiles as of tears, with a strangely pathetic look in them. The prevailing expression of Dr. Joshee's face was grave, dignified, almost sad, but the rare smile which marked her appreciation of the ludicrous was charmingly bright and girlish. The talk drifted during the evening into channels which in spite of her modest diffidence drew her out.

"The car of Juggernaut was discussed, and in speaking of the mothers who distraught with poverty sometimes throw their babes into the Ganges, Dr. Joshee said that during her medical experience in Philadelphia a large number of new-born infants, either murdered or deserted, found their way into the dissecting-room, and she might as well on her return to India relate this fact, making it a *custom* of American mothers to kill or desert their children, and adducing it as a result of Christian belief, as to charge the Hindu faith with the drowning so often reported.

"In discussing the right of men to kill and eat animals, Dr. Joshee said that she had lived in America for three years without feeling the need of any other food than that she ate in India. In speaking of Edwin Arnold's Poems, by which she meant the 'Song Celestial' and 'Indian Idylls' she said he had not, exaggerated but had sometimes failed to catch the subtle spiritual meanings of the ancient writings."

Of the "Light of Asia," a Buddhist poem, her judgment would probably have been different. The King of Siam, in writing to the author to confer upon him the "Order of the White Elephant," says, "I can see that some of your ideas are not the same as ours;" and when Mr. Arnold visited Ceylon, the Chief Priest said to him, "The reason that we wish to honour you is because you have helped to make Buddhists know how much they ought to do and be to rise to the level of their own religion."

"She spoke sensibly of 'Christian Science,' said she had taken several lessons in that art of healing, and thought she saw a natural basis on which it could be explained. She spoke of phrenology, and said that in dissecting the brain she had found reason to dispute the claims made by its enthusiastic advocates.

"Her acquaintance with American and English scientists and persons of note was something phenomenal. As she glanced over a large collection of portrait photographs, a word or two would show that she was familiar with the story of each man and his work."

The friends of Anandabai are grateful for the brief record here preserved. There is no adequate representation of her varied and stimulating conversation. In reference to what she said of diet, she was doubtless glad to reinforce her husband's opinion; but I think it certain that if she could have taken animal food, or at least broths, her chance of life in this climate would have been greater.

It was only a few days before I saw Anandabai, that at the meeting of the Free Religious Association in Boston, during the last week in May, Gopal Vinyak Joshee had delivered an address which must deeply have pained her. In this address he asserted that "Christianity lacks every noble attribute; that we are told we must believe as the Christians do, or be immediately damned; that this is not done by one sect but by all, including the broad Unitarian." He charged further that Christianity lacked justice, righteousness, and humanity; that charity was absent through the length and breadth of Christendom; that Moses and Jesus imposed upon the credulity of their followers; and he sustained these statements by arguments as incoherent as they were absurd. Had they been those of a bewildered American, no one would have thought of them twice, but as the first definite expression known to the audience of Hindu thought, they had a certain interest. Anandabai was of course busied with her duties at the Hospital, but she who had no "need of words" could not fail to know in what mood her husband went to that meeting, and to suffer for it. No one knew better than he in his saner moods that to be true his statements needed modifications that he did not give, and that it was the same human frailty that made his own country people worship idols, and not Christianity, that should be made to answer for the failures of the church. Now that we know that Anandabai was never to devote a life-time to medical work, it is impossible not to wish that she had left the operating-room that day, and carried her own message to that meeting. How tenderly and with what true appreciation would she have spoken of her own indebtedness to Christian charity, justice, and sympathy. "I am not a Christian because I have no need to be one," she would have said; "but it is through Jesus that God has spoken to you. If I do not need your Bible, neither do you need my Shasters."

While she was in Philadelphia she had become acquainted with the Rev. Charles G. Ames. Between him and her there was no "need of words." She entered into his spirit, and it was her greatest delight to listen to his preaching in Spring Garden Street.

"She was often at the church," writes Mr. Ames, "and showed her interest by lingering long at the close, and accepting with sweet and gracious silence, and hand pressure, all the greetings of the people. It was not customary for her to initiate conversation, but once engaged, she talked remarkably well, and generally on serious subjects. She was a guileless and genuine person who knew her own mind and saw clearly 'the path.' Her capacity for self-direction, coupled with rare and generous justice, promised a career of great usefulness in her native land, where, alas! her countrywomen will never know their loss."

It was one of the great disappointments of her brief stay in Boston that she had no opportunity to make the acquaintance of James Freeman Clarke. She had read his books and liked them. If she had been well, she would have gone to see him. She did not like to return to India without meeting him.

Her disappointment in connection with the work at the Hospital was much greater than she ever acknowledged. She had the highest opinion of its administration.

I went from Boston to Concord early in July. I heard there of the address delivered by Gopal one day in June at Mr. Chamberlain's, regarding missionary life in India. This address was written out for the "Index" of July 22d, 1886. Can any one who reads it believe it to be the production of a sane man, provided that man be, as Gopal Joshee undoubtedly was, both cultivated and intelligent?

Forgetting what he had said at the Free Religious meeting in May, he said here, "I do not speak against Christ and his teachings, but I find his followers unworthy of the name;" and goes on: "I have been with missionaries for the last twenty-two years. The more I look into their characters, the darker is the dye that stains them." "Christians have manufactured all the vices, and exported them to countries where simplicity and innocence reigned," — and to confirm his charges against the missionaries, he would have us believe that in travelling to this country with his wife, some of them put meat into her plate, to force her through hunger to break the requirements of her caste!

If all the rest of the world had reason to complain of the church, what right had Gopal Joshee to make such complaint? It was a missionary of the Presbyterian Church who came to his aid and forwarded his letters to Dr. Wilder, when he first desired to send his wife to America. It was Mr. and Mrs. Thorburn, missionaries at Calcutta, who watched over her and protected her, when with insane precipitation her husband would have sent her to this country alone. It was the authorities of the Baptist College, in the town consecrated to Henry Martyn's memory, who granted their hall to Anandabai, when the clamor of the natives at Serampore interfered with the transaction of the public business. It was under the convoy of missionaries that she finally came to America; and the friends who received and cherished her in Roselle and Philadelphia were Christians, and others were clergy of the "broad Unitarian" church. If there had been a spark of nobleness in this Gopal's breast, would he not have known how to tell his truth without repulsing his best friends?

Some one, at the close of the lecture, asked Mr. Joshee if what he had said of the Missionaries applied to Mr. Dall. He hesitated a moment, and then said "I do not know Mr. Dall." And yet, when a month later the news of Mr. Dall's death had come, he wrote to me that I could not imagine "how much he was beloved in India!"

It happened about this time that Mr. Joshee and Anandabai were invited to attend a missionary meeting a few miles from New York. The friends whom they were visiting accompanied them with fear and trembling, having frequently heard Gopal express himself as he did in his letter to "The Index;" but to their surprise, he delivered a delightful address which pleased everybody. He told pleasant stories, described the missionary buildings and schools, and was loudly applauded.

"What does this mean, Mr. Joshee?" said one of his friends, indignant at what she considered his duplicity. "How does this agree with what you were telling me last night?" "I must tell them what they want to hear," said he, as if it were a point of manners; "this is what they were expecting!"

Such transparent manœuvring would hardly seem worth while, and this matter concerns us only as it affected the health and spirits of Dr. Joshee. Obediently she went with her husband to Concord, sitting by him throughout his long tirade, silent and suffering. "She does not look very attractive," said a lady in the audience, "but I wish she would tell us what *she* thinks."

On the first of July she reached Roselle. Her friends there saw that something needed to be done, but a thorough medical examination does not seem to have been thought of.

Finally, Dr. Joshee started on the 10th of July with Mrs. Carpenter's oldest daughter on a journey to Delaware County, New York. Here the elevation was about fifteen hundred feet above the sea-level. Whether her lungs were in a condition to bear the sudden change from the lowlands of New Jersey may be doubted. The first day she complained of pain and nausea. The next she was better and wrote:—

"We are having lovely times. I have not botanized, but we roam about and work. Sometimes we find nice little strawberry patches and we eat of the fruit heartily. The day before yesterday Eighmie and I went to Aunt Jenny's. I took my 'crazy' work with me, and made one block."

But this cheerful strain could not last. On the 20th of July these words came to Mrs. Carpenter: —

"How I wish you were here. I won't stay much longer, for I have been ill ever since I came. I am having chills three times a day, and fever. My whole body is aching. If you do not come within a reasonable time, I shall leave this place and go to you. I am afraid I shall not see you much before I go to India."

In this letter she mentions having been for ten hours in attendance on a difficult delivery. On the 23d she continues: —

"I am now having two chills daily, and fever after each one. My throat is so inflamed that it keeps me coughing all the time. Last night I did not have five minutes' rest."

It is evident that she had been for some time a victim of malaria, but had not had enough vitality to develop chills. As soon as the invigorating quality of the mountain air made itself felt, they were exhibited. Her husband now went to her, and in a few days the Carpenters followed. It had been all along intended that Dr. Bodley,

Dr. Joshee, and Ramabai should go from Rochester about this time to Niagara, Cincinnati, and Chicago, perhaps even to St. Louis. So little did those who loved Anandabai best, realize her condition, that it was thought this long and exhausting journey might benefit her. When Mrs. Carpenter reached her, in Delaware County, she found her bright and cheerful, but with a troublesome cough. Anandabai was busy putting together a silk quilt, the various blocks of which had been contributed by her American friends. In spite of all that she and her friends could do it could not be finished, and was laid aside till her return to Roselle. She knew that Hospital work would leave her no time for it in India.

Dean Bodley, who never loses an opportunity to advance the interests of women, had forwarded an account of the graduation exercises in Philadelphia to her Majesty Queen Victoria, who has been supposed, possibly with injustice, to disapprove of the medical education of women. Early in August Dr. Bodley received in acknowledgment of her communication the following letter from Sir Henry Ponsonby, the Queen's Private Secretary.

It was addressed to the British legation in this country.

FROM WINDSOR July 14th, 1886.

I am commanded by the Queen to request that you will kindly thank Dr. Bodley for having sent to her Majesty the account of Dr. Joshee's graduation at the Woman's Medical College of Pennsylvania, and to assure you that the Queen has read it with much interest.

On the ninth of August, Anandabai went to Rochester. Her husband had gone a few days in advance, and two days after Mrs. Carpenter received the following touching letter: —

ROCHESTER, N. Y., Aug. 10th, 1886.

MY DEAR AUNT, — I arrived at the station at 9.05 P. M. and at this place at 10.10 P. M. I had a very pleasant and comfortable journey. I was not at all sick, and did not cough more than six or seven times. I was not at all hungry, and ate nothing until after 7 o'clock. Mr. Joshee did not come to meet me in time, but it was not his fault. I wrote him that the train arrived at 9.55, so he did not start till after I had arrived. I inquired at the station and took the tramway near it. I told the conductor where I wanted to go. He told me where to change cars and where to walk on the street. Every house was dark and I could not tell where I was.

Finally I found some people sitting on a piazza, and asked them what number their house bore.

They said seventy, so I turned and went back. Mr. Joshee came in forty minutes after I found the house. I had a terrible coughing spell in the street car. I found a white piece which I thought was five cents, and dropped it in. The good driver looked in the box and asked me if I had put in some money. I said, Yes, when he showed me that I had put in 25 cents. He was very sorry, and so was I, but I did not say anything. The honest driver could not open the box, but he managed so nicely that I got twenty cents back. A gentleman who stepped in was told by the driver of my mistake and paid me his fare; nor did the driver let anybody put in another fare till I had my twenty cents back. I could not help feeling extremely grateful to the stranger for his kindness. My impression is that the drivers are honest. This is the way I have always found people. My experience is better than Timon's.

I can't write any better and cough too.

Affectionately yours,

ANANDABAI.

On the 20th of August the following letter came to Mrs. Carpenter, but not in Anandabai's handwriting. It was dictated to her companion, and shows an utter self-forgetfulness, in the deadly grasp of her disease. Dr. Bodley found herself unable to take the journey, for which she probably considered Anandabai unfit. This settled,

Anandabai planned with cheerful courage for herself, and strove in this her last struggle against fate to gratify the trivial but natural curiosity of those she met.

ROCHESTER, Aug. 18th, 1887.

MY DEAR AUNT, — Your letters are at hand. Dr. Bodley is not able to go with me, so I shall leave Rochester for the Falls on the 20th. Mr. Joshee will go with me as far as the Falls. He will put me in the cars for Chicago, where my friend will meet me. She will show me everything worth seeing in that City. From Chicago I shall buy a ticket to Warrensburg, Missouri, where Dr. Smith will meet me. I shall leave Dr. Smith to go to Cincinnati, where I shall meet Dr. Bodley. Will you be kind enough to send my red silk saree which is in the trunk, and either my shawl or my graduating dress? My friends are so disappointed that I have not any pretty dresses with me! and Dr. Smith wants me to bring some pretty sarees. They will not get lost if they are expressed. My cough is not any better. Love to all.

In some way Dr. Bodley forced her own plans to bend to Anandabai's need, for before Anandabai could start she joined her with Ramabai at Rochester, and it was at once decided that the Western journey must not be undertaken.

They determined to go to the Falls and from thence to Philadelphia, that Anandabai might have rest and treatment at the Woman's Hospital. At Carlisle, on the route to Philadelphia, there is an Indian school superintended by my friend Capt. Pratt, under the auspices of the United States Government. Dr. Joshee felt the most intense interest in everything relating to the colored races in this country, and had long desired to visit this especial school, where Indian youth of both sexes are trained in such practical knowledge as will fit them for civilized life.

In spite of such terrible suffering as her disease now involved, her interest did not flag, and it was to gratify her that it was decided to stop at Carlisle on the way to Philadelphia. On the 27th of August I received in Buffalo a line or two dictated by Anandabai, and written by Dr. Bodley in the Central Depot, where they were obliged to wait more than an hour for a train that would go direct to Carlisle. Why could I not have met her and gone with her? Had I done so, I should have endeavored to prevent her immediate departure, and the terrible suffering of the journey to India might have been averted.

She greatly enjoyed her brief glimpse of the Carlisle school. After remaining for ten days at the Woman's Hospital in Philadelphia, Ramabai carried her home to Roselle.

Here her last month in America was to be spent. She fully believed that there was a chance of restoration in the sea-voyage and her native air; but a few words spoken at Roxbury showed me that if the end came, she was ready. To her the thought of death was not —

> "So much even as the lifting of a latch,
> Only a step into the open air,
> Out of a tent already luminous
> With light that shone through its transparent walls."

These words, taken from Longfellow's "Golden Legend," had their origin in the fervid imagination of Father Taylor, but they would have dropped naturally from Anandabai's lips. She had come to see clearly through those "transparent walls," and the most bigoted missionary might have been content to hear her say, "Write me as one who loves her fellow-men." She expected if she reached Bombay alive to go first to Nassik, where her husband's mother resided, and make arrangements for the removal of the whole family to Kolhapur, where she intended to provide for them. Fresh anxieties would wait upon this step, for Nassik is the centre of Brahminism in the Bombay Presidency. She put them steadily aside, determined to cast no wilful shadow over the last days with those she loved.

Of those days Mrs Carpenter shall tell the story.

"Her strength was so far reduced that during the four weeks that she remained with us the greater part of the time was spent in bed or on the lounge, although she generally joined us at lunch or dinner. With her husband, her cousin, and Mr. Sattay in the house, there was everything to make her last days here as comfortable as her condition would allow, and in the merry social converse, in which she eagerly joined, she would have forgotten that she was an invalid, had it not been for the frequent and periodical taking of medicine.

"At no time did any of the 'gloom' of the sick-room attend her. Everything was done to make those precious days as bright and cheerful as possible. It was too hard to believe that all the efforts of her physicians would be in vain, and we tried to shut our eyes to the heart-rending truth."

When the packing was all done, of the eleven trunks, eight contained nothing but souvenirs, and the remaining three held a goodly proportion of the same. Into one of these had gone the silk quilt which Anandabai's loving heart had made a last effort to put together. Dr. Joshee's skill in sewing was something unusual among her countrywomen, and was perhaps due to the Mission school in Bombay. The Hindu dress requires few stitches, and embroidery and ornamental work are usually done by men.

Dr. Joshee had dreaded this final packing, but when the hour for it came, all she could do was to lie still and look on.

"The morning of Oct. 9th, 1886, dawned bright and clear. The carriage was ordered half an hour in advance of the train," Mrs. Carpenter goes on to say, "that Anandabai might see once more every home that had been open to her, and take a last look at that she had called her own. The bright sun and the soft air were not too bright or soft for this parting hour. The motion of the cars made her uncomfortable, and she leaned on my shoulder for support until we reached the carriage in New York. This took us to the 'Etruria.' She was very weak, but sat firmly in her seat as we drove, looking almost as bright as the flowers she carried. She was glad to lie down as soon as we reached the steamer. Not for a moment did she give way. A struggle between her weak body and her strong soul had been going on for days."

The party that accompanied Dr. Joshee to the steamer consisted only of Mrs. Carpenter, her husband, and two children, the Pundita Ramabai, and Mr. Sattay, the Hindu friend who had been with them all during the last weeks. To the last moment these friends, forgetting their grief, occupied themselves with the doctor, stewardess, and others, in arrangements for the invalid's comfort. The purser and steward had been instructed by the agent of the line to show Dr. Joshee special favor in regard to diet, and the physician in charge promised watchful care.

During the month that preceded Anandabai's departure, I heard from Gopal twice, but he wrote about articles that were to be sent to her from Washington, and not one serious word was written about Anandabai's health. In July she had written from Delaware County, "I am coughing with each turn of my pen." In August she adds: —

"I have not as much strength as when I left Delaware County. I do not feel able to go to Chicago, and after rest and care shall go home. Do not worry, for there is no need at all."

From Philadelphia she once wrote: —

"Even the least breeze seems to abuse me. No one in the house realizes the trouble as my Doctor and I do, and no one need.

"My headache, which is reflex, is perfectly intolerable. It is aggravated by every attempt to think."

When I connect the allusions to her health in my own letters with the fuller extracts furnished from Mrs. Carpenter's, I feel sure that Anandabai was not deceived as to her own condition.

For the details of her journey we are obliged to depend on her husband's letters.

He writes first from the steamer "Etruria," Oct. 11th, two days after they had set sail. The weather had been rough, and Dr. Joshee had not left her bed. The Doctor and all the officers were very attentive. On the 13th she had a very bad night, and required the constant attendance of her husband and the physician. Gopal writes that he "prayed to God for mercy."

In the morning she was lifted from her bed that it might be aired, but could not bear the sofa even for a moment. An opiate was given.

A severe storm followed, and when they reached Liverpool on the morning of the 17th Anandabai was almost hopeless, and Gopal was much exhausted by the unusual labors of a nurse, — labors from which, oddly enough if we look at it from a religious point of view, every high caste male Hindu is taught to shrink.

Our next information comes through a very

painful letter published in "The Index" of Dec. 23d, 1886, and which must have been written, one would hope, when Gopal's mind was sore distraught.

In this letter he writes :—

"We are as you know vegetarians. On board the 'Etruria' especial attention was paid to our food. The chief steward sent us any quantity of grapes, apples, pears, and peaches, beside vegetable soups, baked apples, and tomatoes, ice-creams and puddings. On that steamer we were respected.

"We came from New York to Liverpool well cared for and looked after. The Doctor on board called twice a day. The steward and stewardess were always in attendance whenever the bell rang.

"While Dr. Joshee was in America, and up to the time of her landing in England, she never knew what kind of animosity was fostered by the English between the black and white races. She had lived among white people for nearly four years respectfully treated as a lady."

And yet how bitterly Gopal had upbraided her friends in America for not showing sufficient consideration for her race and habits!

They had sailed from New York Oct. 9th, and reached London Oct. 18th, if I can trust Mr. Joshee's figures.

The temptation to quote the whole of this letter is strong, for in no other way could I so fully justify to my reader what I have felt it necessary to indicate of Mr. Joshee's temper and excitable nature; but I forbear.

Thomas Cook & Son, who booked Mr. and Mrs. Joshee from New York to Bombay, had secured by telegraph a berth in the British Steamer "Hergoda." On their arrival in London on the 18th, their baggage was immediately transferred at a heavy expense to this steamer. Gopal then went to the office of Cook & Co. to ascertain exactly when the steamer would sail. He wished to leave the country as soon as possible, being sure, he says, that if he did not he should be "imprisoned for life" or "committed to the gallows"!!! Cook & Co. could not furnish the information he wanted, and he was sent to the office of the British India Steamship Co. Here he was refused a ticket on the ground that the passage money was not yet paid, and they would not grant it now that they knew the passenger would be a Hindu lady. "I was all wrath and indignation," Mr. Joshee goes on, "I burst, as is my wont, into bitter exclamations. I abused the English right and left, and said that their houses in India should be blown up, and every insult retaliated by bloodshed." Such words as these, and the far worse words that followed, could hardly have availed to secure the accommodation that he wanted. It is impossible to understand this story as Gopal tells it. Hindu passengers and European passengers of every rank are constantly making the passage from India to England and back in the same vessel, and there is nothing in the public opinion of England to sustain the outrage here described.

Mr. Joshee does not forget to tell us that in this sharp trial Anandabai remained "firm as a rock." When he returned to the hotel, he met there two ladies, who, unable to believe the story, went to the office of Cook & Co. The next day, the 20th of October, Mr. Joshee called on the husband of one of these ladies, and on finding what was necessary to enable the travellers to take the outgoing P. & O. steamer which was to sail on the 21st, Mr. Pattison handed Mr. Joshee "a check for eighty or ninety pounds." Is it not a little singular that Gopal does not remember *which?* In speaking of Mrs. Pattison Mr. Joshee says, "Her words at parting were more consoling and redeeming than all the dollars Mrs. Joshee received as presents from her American friends in pomp." These words are printed and I cannot pass them by. Not only did Dr. Joshee receive many gifts from the ladies of Philadelphia, but many benefactions were offered to her husband for her sake, and with a delicacy which hid from every "left hand" what the "right hand" did.

From this moment, if we are to believe Mr. Joshee, everything went ill with the travellers until they reached Bombay. Dr. Joshee was rudely treated by the steward and the subordinates on board the "Peshawur." Mr. Joshee had made one serious mistake at the outset, in booking himself as the servant of his wife. He gives no reason for this, save lack of funds and "curiosity." Why there should have been any "lack of funds" it is difficult to understand. The Dewan of Kolhapur was to pay all the expenses of the new superintendent of the Albert Edward wards, and the large amount of money known to have passed into Mr. Joshee's hands, makes it impossible to understand why he could not pay his own passage. His wife was far too ill to be left alone at night or to be without an attendant of her own sex. If by "curiosity" is meant a desire to see how much irritation and ill-will he could excite by his own violence and perversity, we cannot deny that his experiment succeeded. I take comfort in believing that this letter never met Anandabai's eyes. I remember the sweet tones of her voice as she said soon after her arrival in this country, "I know there are many good husbands in the United States. I see that they make their wives happy. But among them all there is not one so good as my husband." If this letter had come into her hands, she would have seen in it many statements that she would never have authorized. I am glad that this pang was not added to all the rest.

Indirectly we heard that Anandabai took cold in a severe storm in the Bay of Biscay, and reached Gibraltar in a very critical state. From Gibraltar Mr. Joshee goes on:—

"The day we left London Dr. Joshee felt bright, and was able to go on deck without assistance. I, being only her native servant, had to stay away till sent for. The second day she sat there reading. Now she is again confined to her bed, as ill as she was when she last reached Roselle. Now I am with her day and night, and she will soon be better. The sea is calm; it troubles us far less than the people."

In this letter came a few lines from Anandabai to Mrs. Carpenter, the last she ever wrote.

"I am stronger," she says, "cough better, throat worse. I shall improve when I am able to eat. There has not been an hour since I left New York when I have not missed your precious self. I am writing in bed, and see my Doctor twice a day."

At Malta they paused a little while to take in water, fruit, and vegetables.

Mr. Joshee complains of the diet on board this steamer; but neither ice nor fruit is sufficiently cheap in London for the company to supply the P. & O. steamers as they do those of the Cunard line, and for that reason travellers usually supply their own delicacies. On the third of November they entered the Suez Canal. Twelve days ought to take them to Bombay. Anandabai grew hopeful again, and mentioned, her husband says, "a thousand and one things that she would like to eat." The three days in the Red Sea were intensely hot, and at a great risk Anandabai's warmest wraps were removed. Her cough was severe, and she seems to have been wholly sustained by stimulants.

Mr. Joshee alludes in a letter from Aden to various annoyances arising from their color, and adds that an unknown friend on board, who had heard of their trouble in London, sent to offer them money if they needed it. "Patient of hardships," Anandabai reached Bombay. The letters which detailed the landing never reached us, but it could not have been later than the 17th of

November. She was received with distinction and extraordinary marks of regard. Those who expected to see her excommunicated and abused, saw on the contrary the eyes of grave men filling with tears as they gazed upon her wasted form, and heard the strong voices of priests and pundits echoing her praises.

She lingered for some time in Bombay or that neighborhood to take the advice of distinguished European physicians.

It must always be remembered to Mr. Joshee's honour, that during this long voyage, in the last half of which Anandabai was certainly fatally ill, he waited upon his wife with devoted tenderness, and she preferred his care to that of every other. The prospect of a life at his side had faded, and ceased to perplex her. She was glad to rest in a love already tested. For many things she must have suffered; but against the customs of his country-people and in spite of the injunctions of his creed, he waited upon her steadily, performing the duties of a servant, and seeming to forget the privileges of his "sex and caste."

It may be said that he did this from necessity, and with an interested intention to save a valuable life, but I think he did it from pure affection. He had done it once before, to my knowledge, when neither necessity nor hope of gain could possibly have influenced him, and when it exposed him, as it did now, to the harshest contumely, to the most bitter scorn.

At Bombay everything was against our unhappy traveller. For two days the pleasant thought that she was at home roused her to a factitious cheerfulness.

Her mother, younger sister, brother, and grandmother came from various directions to meet her. They could not tempt her with the food she had longed for. The friends with whom they stayed were devoted, but their habits were not those of the Mahrattas. They removed from house to house. Their first resting-place was too damp. At the next they were received for a short time only; and when we remember with what promptness Dr. Joshee's practical sense would have conquered all these difficulties had she been well and acting for any one else, we realize how ill she must have been when she lay there quietly, "nothing asking, nothing doubting."

She had not however given up all hope, for she desired that subscriptions should be made to several medical journals in America, the money to be forwarded after she reached Kolhapur. She was impatient to reach Poonah, but at first her physicians would not allow it. This depressed her, and her husband saw her wasting to a shadow, and became more and more uncertain and harassed.

He says he has no time to write. The interest in Dr. Joshee made her a national centre. "All India is in travail for her."

Physicians were often changed. At last one was found who probably saw the case to be hopeless, and consented to her going to Poonah on the 9th of December.

On the 16th Gopal writes:—

"We are now in the place where Dr. Joshee was born. As we came up into the hills, she brightened up. At first her cough was better. We sent for one native doctor in whom we have full confidence, and whose remedies were very gentle, but collapse followed."

The people of Poonah spent hours in praying for her recovery, but they crowded the house and made it difficult to take proper care of her.

"Some come from curiosity, some from sympathy and affection," writes Gopal. "Those who scarcely ever leave their houses come to see her, the good among the orthodox and the superstitious, forgetting that we have been to America. Dr. Joshee's illness is the concern of all. Siva is our God of Death. To appease him, water is gently trickled over his head for hours daily. The people are doing it now. Every day the Brahmins put ashes on Dr. Joshee's forehead, and she touches a bit with her mouth. Columns are printed in the newspapers about her condition. *I* write to you but do you reply to *her*, that she may feel as if the letter were her own. A word from you is a tonic."

On February 10th he can only repeat the same sad story. They moved once or twice in Poonah, and finally went to the old house of Anandabai's great-uncle, where she was born. He was now very aged, and seems to have had a sort of superstitious feeling that the hand which brought her into the world could hold her back from death.

It was about the middle of December that they reached Poonah, where the grandmother who had been her companion when she left Kalyan to follow the fortunes of Gopal Vinayak, the mother whose disapprobation of her career had perhaps led her to send bitter letters to the Missionaries, were ready to receive her. Here the daily papers issued bulletins of her health; here the Brahmo, the Hindu, and the Christian came, regardless of their superstitions, forgetful of their caste, to pray for her who had laid down her life for their sake.

Gopal was now able to leave her with her mother while he went himself to offer sacrifices to the "gods," and to her "guardian planets," to avert their anger and her death. He performed the penance and paid the fees necessary to reinstate Anandabai in her caste, and all the while life was failing.

On the 20th of February it was evident that the end was near; but whatever had befallen her poor body, Anandabai's spirit was serene and sweet. When she found it impossible to eat, Gopal rebuked her mother as if she had not prepared the food with sufficient care. "The food is good," said the poor patient, "it is I who am out of sorts!" She seems to have had occasional convulsions, and to have endured much.

Gopal says of her:—

"She suppressed her groans that others might not suffer. When conscious she was grave, gentle, meditative, and oh! so brave and thoughtful. She never showed the slightest irritability. She was very strict in everything relating to our faith. Do you believe me? It was so. Her maid-servant must not step on the carpet at her bedside, and her water bottles were removed if a European touched them. When I remonstrated against this as a folly in one who had spent years in America, she pleaded that her grandmother, sister, and mother had such an abhorrence of these things, that she must consider them. Properly speaking, *we* were outcasts, but no one reminded us of it.

"A few days ago the 'Pacification of the Waters' was performed for her. Brahmins were seated at dinner, and her old uncle sent for me that I might sprinkle water on the banana leaves on which the food was served. Did they consider me as an outcast when they asked me to do this? Even the reformers are astonished at the manner in which we have been treated by the most orthodox Hindus. We have conquered every enemy but Death."

The Mahratta papers had warned the physicians not to allow their professional jealousy to interfere with "duty to a patient in whom all India felt a national concern." I copy from the Dnyana Chaksu of March 2nd, 1887, the following account, translated by the Pundita Ramabai:—

"Although Anandabai was so young, her perseverance, undaunted courage, and devotion to her husband were unparalleled. It will be long before we again see a woman like her. The education which she had received had greatly heightened her nature and ennobled her mind. Although she suffered more than words can express, from her mortal disease, which was consumption, not a word of complaint or impatience ever escaped her lips. After months of dreadful suffering, she was so reduced that no one could look on her without pain; yet, wonderful to tell, Anandabai thought it her present duty to suffer silently and cheerfully."

It was at midnight on the 26th of February, 1887, that the final call came. The previous night had been one of great suffering; the whole family had been up all night.

Through it all Anandabai's face was bright and she spoke cheerful words to those about her. At ten o'clock, worn out by anxiety and fatigue, Gopal administered some medicine and went to his own bed. At midnight a strong convulsion came on. Anandabai called loudly, but before her mother could lift her to her bosom, the gentle, faithful soul had fled.

Her last audible words were, "I have done all that I could."

"The family then bathed the body and decked it with bright garments and ornaments, according to our Hindu custom," her husband goes on to say. "There was no time to spread the sad news throughout the city, but all who had heard of it, followed her remains to the cremation ground, on the following Sunday, thus showing their respectful affection. Some of us had feared that the priests might object to cremating the body with the sacred fire, according to the Hindu rites, but our fears were groundless. When I offered sacrifices to avert her death, they had gladly officiated, showing a generous liberality."

Anandabai needed neither vows nor sacrifices nor crematory rites to bring her soul to the foot of "The Great White Throne," but she had more than once desired that everything should be done, after her death, to gratify and appease those who still recognized their force.

"It will do me no harm," she said once, when speaking to me of such matters.

After the body was placed upon the funeral pile, Mr. V. M. Ranadè made an oration in Dr. Joshee's honor, and the cremation was then completed.

"But she is dead! that sweet intellectual soul, that large-brained self-forgetful womanly creature — dead at the early age of twenty-one years and eleven months — dead on the threshold of the work for which she was so well equipped!"

There are those of us who loving her tenderly cannot think without pain of the weary journey, undertaken without the needed nurse and companion; but turning our eyes to the country which she loved, and which, because she loved it, she left, turning to the countrywomen whom she died to save, we feel that her death, in sorrow, disappointment, and bodily anguish, will in God's own way accomplish still more than the life for which we prayed.

THE END.